COACHI

SALES SUCCESS

How to Create the
Value Added Sales Culture

Tom Reilly
Author, *Value-Added Selling*

Motivation Press
St. Louis, MO

Library of Congress Cataloging in Publication Data

Reilly, Thomas P.
  Coaching for Sales Success:
  How to Create the Value Added Culture
  ISBN: 0-944448-27-5

Other Books by Tom Reilly:

  Value-Added Selling
  Value Added Sales Management
  Customer Service Is More Than a Department
  Crush Price Objections
  How to Sell and Manage in Tough Times and Tough Markets
  Get Out of the Wagon and Help Me Pull This Thing
  Selling Smart!
  Simple Psychology

Copyright©, 2004 by Tom Reilly
Library of Congress Catalog Card Number: 2004107193
International Standard Book Number: 0-944448-27-5

Printed in the United States of America by Motivation Press.

Dedication

To the little league baseball teams and soccer teams
I coached. These children taught me plenty about coaching.

Acknowledgements

I want to thank Joann Hamilton and Charlotte Reilly
for their ongoing commitment to this project.

Table of Contents

INTRODUCTION

Consider this:

- 56% of salespeople say they are not being coached the right way by their sales managers.
- 57% of salespeople say they want *more* coaching from their sales managers.
- 60% of salespeople say they want *better* coaching from their sales managers.
- A survey of 278 business executives found coaching skills to be the number one characteristic of effective sales managers.
- Only 32% of sales managers are considered outstanding coaches by their salespeople.
- 46% of salespeople say that their sales managers need better management skills.

Wow! I think I made the point. If you are a sales manager, chances are you need help.

Coaches come in all sizes, shapes, and varieties—athletic coaches, teachers, mentors, tutors, band directors, clergy, parents, siblings, vocal coaches, writing coaches, dance teachers, executive coaches, life coaches, fitness coaches, personal trainers, and scout leaders. My little league baseball coach spent more time with us than our losing record warranted. A high school teacher, who happened to be a track coach, saw something positive in me I did not know existed. The graduate student who taught my college composition course sparked a writing fire in me that forged my career. I took golf lessons from a coach who reminded me of my motivational principles when I got discouraged with the lack of results. Not all of my coaches wore a whistle or carried a clip board. Some wore pocket protectors or carried a Music Director's baton. There were a couple of sales managers who believed in me, convinced me that I knew something about sales and could make a living doing it.

Think back to the great coaches in your life. Who were they? What did they do for you? What did they mean to you? They taught you how to play with passion, how to win with grace, and how to fail with dignity. They taught you that victory brings with it the responsibility of leadership and that failure is feedback and only temporary. They built your confidence and tested it from time to time. They gave you a hug when you needed it and a kick in the backside when you needed that. Your great coaches did what all great coaches do: They put the spotlight on you, not themselves.

Great coaches put the spotlight on others, not themselves.

I coached youth soccer and little league baseball for eleven years—many of those years as a training league coach for the youngest of players. One of my players was born with a congenital hip problem, which meant he ran oddly. As children do, others made fun of his unorthodox running style. After practice one day, his mother came up to me and said, "Tom, you know the other kids at school make fun of John and the way he runs. He came home the other day and said, 'Mom, the kids made fun of me again today on the playground because of my running, but that's okay because Coach Reilly thinks I run just fine.' Thanks, Tom."

I thought I was coaching soccer, but discovered I was really coaching him on how to deal with critics and handle rejection.

Whew! Coaching is an awesome responsibility when you consider the impact you have on other people.

Having trained more than 100,000 salespeople and their managers since 1981, I have witnessed similarities between managers and the parents of the children I coached. Occasionally, I would ask parents for their assistance—time to help out at practice or time to work the concession stands at the game fields. Some offered their time; most offered to "buy out" their commitment. They chose to spend the money versus invest the time. In fairness to those whose work schedules would not allow them to donate time, they contributed what they could. However, there were parents who had the time but did not want to give it to the team or to the athletic association.

Like these parents, I have met plenty of managers and business owners who would rather spend money to fix the sales force's problems than to invest the time to fix the problems themselves. They do not want to do the heavy lifting. They abdicate their responsibility. They ask me, "What will you do to guarantee the success of the training?"

I respond, "What will you do?" These managers often walk at this point because they do not want to do the grunt work of coaching, guiding, and leading their salespeople. They are responsible *for* their salespeople, and I am responsible *to* their salespeople.

I know managers who do not want to take the medicine they are prescribed. In effect, they are asking me, "What will you do to guarantee that I will take the medicine?" They want me to micro manage them to ensure that they do their jobs. Imagine asking your doctor what he or she will do to ensure that you take the medication you are given!

I mention these examples and parallels to point out that there is a huge opportunity for someone that internalizes the coaching function and takes full responsibility for his or her salespeople.

Because many managers would rather pay someone to do this for them, your willingness to do the heavy lifting of coaching, managing and leading your salespeople gives you a significant competitive advantage in the marketplace and generates passionate loyalty among your salespeople.

Why did you buy this book? Did your boss give it to you and tell you to read it? I bet you want to become a great coach, and you see the opportunity in doing so. But, how coachable are you? Are you as coachable a manager as you want your salespeople to be? Success in any profession requires the discipline to do what you know you must do, even and especially when you lack the motivation to do it.

To be an effective coach, you must be willing to do the heavy lifting and invest the time in your employees.

Why is coaching so important? Seventy percent of employees leave their employers because of the manager, the coach. They do not like working for the person they work for. Could this manager be a poor coach? Probably. The average sales force turns over 43% of its salespeople every two years! These salespeople are not all leaving for a better territory or compensation plan. Most leave because of their relationship—or lack of—with their coach, their sales manager.

Consider these reasons for developing your coaching skills:

- Sales managers who follow up on training and coach their salespeople get four times the return on training dollars they invest. This leads to a quicker transfer of skills and greater return on training dollars invested.
- Coaching has been shown to be at least as effective a strategy as training for changing sales behavior. Investing one-on-one time with your salespeople, guiding and

mentoring them, can yield similar if not greater results than sending your salespeople to training.

- Research on Emotional Intelligence shows that as a leader, 70% of your success comes from your ability to manage yourself and your relationships with your subordinates.
- Coaching is the right thing to do; it is a major part of your job. Why did you want to become a sales manager if you did not want to coach your salespeople?
- It is good for the morale of your sales force. They want to spend meaningful time with you. What does it say to your sales force if you spend money but not time with them? Not to overstate this, it is the same dynamic as parents spending time with their children.

Over the years, I have heard the following bogus explanations from sales executives who do not want to make the commitment to coach their salespeople:

"I don't have time for this." This means you have a time management problem *and* a coaching problem. It is a problem of priorities. Imagine saying to your family, "I don't have time for you." If you lack the time to attend to the resources that contribute to your success, on what high-priority activities are you spending your time?

"They should do this on their own." If this is true, your salespeople would be working for themselves and not you. To extend this faulty logic, they do not need you. If your salespeople could view things strategically (your job) and execute tactically (their job), why do they need you? It is like saying, "Our product should be good enough to sell itself." In that case, you do not need a sales force, do you? Salespeople who are so totally self-reliant that they do not require the guidance of a sales manager or a coach are generally self-employed.

"I am not a baby sitter for my people." Coaching is not micro management. This is a negative view of coaching. You view it as punishment for you and the salesperson. How do you think your salesperson views it? To be an effective coach, you must begin thinking in terms of the benefits of coaching.

"I have professional salespeople. They don't need me to coach them. They would resent it." Do you think Tiger Woods resents the input he gets from his coach? Are your salespeople more professional than Tiger? To me, this excuse sounds like the manager attributing his or her views of coaching to the salesperson. We call this projection in psychology.

All of these faulty views of coaching suggest that managers who believe any of these have not taken part in effective coaching—either as a manager or as an employee. Learning how to become a more effective sales coach may help you learn how to get more value from your boss as well.

Coaching is how you bring value to your sales team.

The skills and information that appear in this book can be generally applied to any coaching situation, though they are designed for sales management, specifically value added sales management. There are many books on coaching—managerial, executive level, mentoring, and even sports. This book is designed to help you create the value added sales culture.

I begin by describing the value added sales culture and use it as a backdrop for the rest of the book. To get the most from your salespeople, you must have a vision of where your company is headed and translate that into a unifying mission statement for your sales force that supports your company's goals. Your departmental goals support the company's goals and the sales force's goals support your goals. This linkage—vision to mission to goals—is vital for your success. You develop a strategy for achieving these goals, and your sales force tactically executes this strategy.

Next, we examine the dynamics of your sales management infrastructure. An effective sales management infrastructure begins with recruiting the right people, challenging them with sales objectives, training them to execute the mission, compensating them for their efforts, motivating them, and coaching them to the highest levels. All of this begins with the mission to become a value added sales culture, the core focus of your efforts. It is why you choose the people you recruit, challenge them with the right objectives, train them to achieve these objectives, compensate them accordingly, motivate them to accomplish your mission, and coach them to success.

The last section of this book contains additional readings on relevant sales management topics and exercises for you to conduct with your salespeople to create the value added sales culture in your organization.

Before reading further, please write your objectives for reading this book. What do you want to learn and to accomplish by reading this?

_____

_____

_____

CHAPTER ONE: CULTURE BUILDING

Every company has a culture—an identity, climate, environment, atmosphere, way of life, traditions, and operating paradigms. It is built on attitudes, beliefs, and mores. Some company cultures are product focused; these companies are known for their innovation and commitment to excellence in what they create. The product is the culture. Generally, they are held up as the industry standard. Some companies are service focused; everything they do takes on a service tone. These companies view themselves as relationship managers with customers. Some companies are known as logistics specialists; supply-chain management and operational efficiency are the lifeblood of their organization. Many companies are known as sales organizations; everyone in the company views themselves as salespeople. Their mantra is, "Everyone sells something to someone." Other companies have a technical culture; they are known as "techies." Techies are good at the technical side of the business, but they may not be as good at people issues.

Some organizations are paternalistic; others are entrepreneurial. Some are democratic; others are bureaucratic. Some companies have a family feel to them, even if they are publicly held. Some cultures are customer focused while others are seller focused. Some company cultures are employee friendly while others cater to management. Some company cultures are built around a curiosity about their potential while others look to the marketplace and competitors for performance benchmarks. Even "no culture" is a culture. It is called chaos. You have a culture. Is it the one you want? Will your culture get you to where you want to be?

Cultures attract certain kinds of people. Healthcare, education, business, military, government, manufacturing, religion, retail, sports, and the media draw people who prefer to work in that particular culture. The word that an organization is women-friendly, minority-friendly, or immigrant-friendly spreads fast in the inner circles of those interested in these opportunities.

This chapter is about introspection, insight and culture building. I want to help you get a better view of where you are and where you want to be with your business culture. Beyond insight and understanding, this chapter is about creating the type of sales and sales management culture you want in your company and in your department. For you to achieve your objectives and help your company accomplish its mission, your sales and sales management culture must support these efforts. This chapter is about building a special kind of sales culture, the value added sales culture. Even though you could use these principles to create any sales culture, the value added sales culture serves as the backdrop for the rest of this book.

Focus is positive tunnel vision. It is going an inch wide and a mile deep. It is investing with laser-like intensity your resources and your energy in areas that will give you the return you desire.

For you to achieve your objectives and help your company accomplish its mission, you must leverage your resources fully and cooperatively, in an integrated and coordinated manner. This happens when you direct these resources—people, systems, technology, processes, and equipment—down a path that focuses narrowly on your fundamental purpose for being in business.

Developing a solid and identifiable business culture creates a corporate identity and provides mission clarity. It helps communicate and reinforce your vision throughout the organization. It also sends a consistent message to the marketplace. Your customers and competition know who you are and what you stand for. Internally, this builds employee pride and loyalty. Externally, you broadcast your brand to the industry. Focus, consistency, and discipline will be your best friends in this endeavor.

Your culture affects every aspect of your sales management efforts. From the people you hire, to the sales objectives you set, to the training you design, to the compensation plan you establish, to the coaching you provide, your culture defines your efforts. That is good news. Culture adds purpose, discipline and form to your initiatives.

If your company lacks an identifiable business culture, it shows in employee confusion and frustration. If you lack a sales management infrastructure, you cannot blame your salespeople for a failure to perform. After all, they are following your lead.

Your Culture

Describe your business culture.

_____

_____

_____

What do you want it to look like?

_____

_____

_____

Why?

_____

_____

_____

Do you have a coaching culture?

_____

_____

_____

Why do you want a value added sales culture?

_____

_____

_____

The Value Added Sales Culture

This book is about one type of sales culture—the value added sales culture. Value-Added Selling is more than a book, a training session or a course—it is a course of action. It is a philosophy, paradigm, mindset and process, complete with strategies and tactics. Value-Added Selling begins with simple but powerful attitudes that emanate from a customer-oriented philosophy of serving:

- I seek ways to add value, not cost with my efforts.
- I pursue excellence in all that I do.
- I define and sell value in customer terms.
- I may sell the first experience with my company, but it is the total experience with my company that encourages customers to return.
- I sell value, not price.

Pre-Sale	Transition	Post-Sale
Planning	**Acquisition**	**Usage**
During Planning, the buyer's greatest need is for information. They study their needs, source a solution, and select the best alternative. Their critical activities include needs assessment, setting priorities and objectives, establishing budgets, etc.	During Acquisition, the buyer's greatest need is for smooth, seamless, and painless transitions. Their critical activities include placing orders, receiving goods, redistribution, handling credits, returns, etc.	During Usage, the customer's greatest need is for maximum performance, productivity, and economy. Their critical activities include usage and disposal.

Offensive Selling Mode		Defensive Selling Mode	
Pursuing new business		**Protecting existing business**	
Focusing	**Persuading**	**Supporting**	**After-Marketing**
During this phase of the sales process you identify viable sales opportunities, qualify these opportunities, penetrate the accounts thoroughly, and develop an in-depth understanding of the customer's needs, wants, and concerns. You take this information and brainstorm a solution. **You're in the diagnostician role.**	This is the phase of the sale where you polish your image, create distance between you and the competition and convince the customer that your product or service is *the* value added solution. **You're in the promoter role.**	During this phase of the sale you follow up to ensure that the customer experiences smooth transitions to your solution, receives special attention as needed, and builds strong relationship ties. **You're in a service and logistics support role.**	This is the sale-after-the-sale: the phase when you look for ways to continue to add value, get credit for what you do, and grow your business. You're an advocate for the customer and liaison for your company. You help monitor their inventory and usage. **You're in the growth mode.**

Illustration 1-1: The Value Added Sales Process™

In a value added sales culture, the sales manager builds his or her infrastructure around these attitudes. The people you recruit, the objectives you set, the training you provide, how you compensate your salespeople, and how you motivate and coach them all focus on these Value-Added Selling attitudes. After all, that is your core focus.

There are two points worth mentioning about the Value Added Sales Process™ (see illustration 1-1). First, this is a customer-driven sales process; it parallels the buyer's Critical Buying Path™ (the steps buyers go through from the moment a need exists, up to and including complete need satisfaction). This cradle-to-grave model offers many opportunities for your company to add value with your products, services and salespeople. For every step along the buyer's path, there is an equivalent step for the salesperson to add value.

Value added salespeople move at about the same speed and on parallel tracks with their customers.

Second, the Value Added Sales Process™ is different because of the emphasis we place on defensive selling—the sale-after-the-sale. Value-Added Selling respects follow-up as much as lead generation. This means your sales culture, if it is to become a value added sales culture, must reinforce defensive selling with performance objectives and compensation. Salespeople move in the direction of their rewards. As a manager, you cannot pay lip service to the value added sales culture and expect positive results. Customer retention and growth (defensive selling) are at least as important to you as customer acquisition (offensive selling). If your company suffers from pipeline-itis, an obsession with acquiring new customers, you will find that Value-

Added Selling challenges your most fundamental beliefs about business and sales.

Sales Management Infrastructure

In this section, I give a brief explanation of the dynamics of a typical sales management infrastructure, saving most of my comments for the individual chapters. If you want your sales management culture to reinforce Value-Added Selling, you must invest time, energy, and resources in each of these areas:

Selection and recruiting—every coach looks at his or her team, determines its strengths and weaknesses and then attempts to fill the gaps by recruiting the right kind of talent. You must recruit and hire salespeople who can help you achieve your mission to build a value added sales force.

Setting objectives—once you have recruited the right talent, you must establish value added sales objectives that support your company's mission and your departmental goals. These sales objectives become performance standards for your sales force.

Training and Development—you have recruited the right talent and focused them with value added sales objectives. Now, prepare them for the challenge. It is unreasonable for you to assume that hiring even the most experienced salesperson excuses your responsibility for training them.

Compensation—you have recruited the right talent, focused them with value added sales objectives and provided them with training. Now, concentrate on rewarding them for accomplishing their goals. This is one of the shortest chapters in this book because most sales managers who attend my coaching seminars can do little about their compensation plans. But I would be remiss if I did not offer some fundamental thoughts and questions on compensation.

Motivation—you have recruited the right talent, focused them with value added sales objectives, provided them with training, and built a compensation plan that supports your value added sales objectives. Now, tap into their motivation-to-achieve. Motivation is the energy that impels action. It is the result of a blend of internal and external forces. Every successful sales coach is a master motivator.

Coaching—you have recruited the right talent, focused them with value added sales objectives, provided them with training, built a compensation plan that supports your value added sales objectives, and developed a deep understanding of what motivates your troops. Now, it is time to coach your people to their potential. This chapter is probably the reason you picked up this book. Read patiently to get to this chapter so that you understand all the steps on this journey.

How does your sales management infrastructure compare to this model?

_____

_____

_____

Get the MOST™ From Your Sales Force

As your sales force achieves its value added sales objectives, you accomplish your departmental objectives, and your company achieves its goals and accomplishes its mission. This is no accident. Organizational success is the natural outcome of individual and team success. To get the most from your sales force, you must begin with a vision.

A vision is a dream, a calling, a view of the future—what's to come—governing values, purpose, what you stand for, what you stand against, direction, destiny, guiding principles, center, core, compass, what you live for and maybe what you die for. Effective planning begins with a vision of what is to become. That vision, translated into a mission, unifies a team and gives it the direction to succeed. Most companies fail because they begin their plan with goals instead of a vision and a mission. Here is how to get the MOST™ from your sales team.

Mission—this is the *why* behind your goals. It is why your goals make sense. If your mission is to become known as *the* customer-friendly company in your industry, customer satisfaction and retention goals make sense. This is built on a vision that if you respect people and treat them well, you will dominate in the future because your industry is moving in a different, less friendly direction.

Objectives—these are *what* you want to achieve. Goals are proof that you are accomplishing your mission. They are the sign posts along your journey. If market dominance via customer-friendly service is the mission, a customer retention rate of 95% is a worthy goal.

Strategies—these are what you must do to reach your customer retention goals. They may include re-writing sales objectives to reflect your efforts at defensive selling. They could include changing your compensation plan to reflect account retention and training your salespeople on defensive selling.

Tactics—these are the day-to-day tasks that your salespeople perform to execute your defensive selling strategy and reach your customer retention goals and accomplish your mission. It is how you must do what you must do.

Whew! That sounds like a lot of work, doesn't it? Not really. A lack of structure makes your task more challenging and frustrating. This model adds discipline and form to your efforts.

It provides direction and coordination. It takes the guesswork out of sales management and coaching. Everything you do from hiring, to setting objectives, to training, to compensating, to motivating, to coaching is directed with singleness-of-purpose. How simple can it get?

If you want to build a value added sales force, begin with a vision of what it will look like. Translate that vision into a mission statement. Set objectives that signal you are on the right path. Develop strategies to direct your resources. Coach your salespeople on the tactical execution of your strategy. This is how to get the MOST™ from your salespeople.

If you want to build a value added sales management infrastructure, make sure you attend to these six critical dynamics: recruiting and selection, setting objectives, training and development, compensation, motivation, and coaching. Let Value-Added Selling be your focus for this process. Staff for it. Set goals for it. Train for it. Pay for it. Motivate for it. Coach for it.

What is your vision for your company?

_____

_____

_____

Translate that vision into a mission statement.

_____

_____

_____

What departmental objectives support this mission?

_____

_____

_____

What strategies must you employ to achieve your departmental objectives?

_____

_____

_____

What tactics must your sales force employ (to execute your strategies) to achieve your departmental objectives and to accomplish your mission?

_____

_____

_____

Summary

Every company has a culture—even no culture is a culture. Your company has a culture. Do you know what it is? The value added sales culture serves as a backdrop for this book. An effective sales management infrastructure has six critical dynamics: recruiting, goal setting, training and development, compensation, motivation, and coaching. To get the MOST™ from your sales group, begin with a vision, translate it into a mission statement, establish objectives that support the mission, and design strategies and tactics to achieve your goals. Your salespeople should execute tactically what you design strategically.

To get the most value from this chapter, write your action steps for using these ideas.

_____

_____

_____

CHAPTER TWO:
RECRUITING AND SELECTION

Consider this:

- The average sales force turns over by 43% every two years.
- 80% of the salespeople currently employed in sales are in the wrong sales position or are selling the wrong product.

Hiring is today's dominant concern. In my seminars and in my casual conversations with sales managers, I often hear this question, "Where do I find great sales talent?" Every coach wants to know the secret for discovering talent, as if there is a magical formula for identifying and attracting top talent.

If you are a sales manager and salespeople report to you, your fundamental job responsibility is recruiting top talent for your sales team.

New coaches evaluate talent, identify gaps or holes in their system or team and attempt to fill them. Coaching begins with talent—using what you have and attracting new talent. This is Step One in achieving your sales management objectives and accomplishing your company's mission—lining up and maximizing the talent.

This chapter is about sales management infrastructure Dynamic Number One: Identifying what you need in a team, defining what you need in jobs for the team, understanding what you need in candidates to fill the jobs for your team, assessing the talent you currently have in place, and recruiting potential candidates who fit these needs and fill the gaps.

More Than a Warm Body in a Hot Territory

Often, I hear from sales managers, "I just need to get a body in the territory." That's pathetic! How lazy can you get! If you believe that all you need is a warm body, you are on a short trip to nowhere. It is like saying to a salesperson, "I don't care how you get the business or what you do, just bring me an order."

What does this warm-body-in-a-hot-territory say to customers? To me, it sounds like you are saying, "We really don't care enough about your business to hire the best; we're just filling a job vacancy."

How does hiring a warm body help your company achieve maximum territory potential? Are you going to get maximum leverage from this sales territory? Will mediocre sales performance help you achieve your departmental objectives and company mission? Do you have mediocre goals? Do you want to be known as the company that hires the most *average* people in the industry? You need more than a warm body in a hot territory. Your customers deserve better than this. Your company deserves better than this. You deserve better than this.

The people you hire help you achieve your company's mission, meet your departmental objectives, and most importantly serve as your personal launching pad for your future success. Imagine attempting to get to the Super Bowl, World Cup Soccer, World Series or Stanley Cup with the most mediocre talent you can find. Do you go to the symphony for the best *average* music they can play? When you go to the dentist, do you hope he or she has hired the best dental technician to work on your teeth? When you call a technical service help line, do you want to speak to *just* a voice or to the best available technician?

Your customers and your company deserve the best. It is your job, as sales manager—the coach—to make this happen. You may have to fight for the resources to achieve this goal. You may have to search long and hard to find the right person. You may have to wait a little longer than you wanted to fill the slot, but you definitely want more than a warm body in a hot territory.

This book is about building a value added sales culture, staffed with salespeople that embrace and act on this mission. Your culture is your corporate identity. Your market identifies your company with the type of people you hire. Your salespeople are walking billboards for your company. You could invest millions of dollars to create an image in the marketplace, but the minute your salespeople show up at the customers' doorsteps, they either confirm or negate the image you carefully crafted. View your sales force through the prism of what it takes to be known as the value added sales organization. View your sales force as a vital part of your marketing plan. They should be the most dynamic part of it, not the weakest.

Job Analysis and Strategic Staffing

Recruiting talent begins by your studying the demands of the sales job. What types of sales jobs do you need to staff to achieve your department's objectives and to accomplish your company's mission? I like to use a military analogy to describe this process. If you were charged with taking a hilltop position, what types of soldiers and weapons would you need to accomplish the mission? Would you require snipers, ground assault, automatic-weapons specialists, mortars, armor, artillery, and air support?

As sales manager—the coach—you must direct your available resources toward achieving organizational objectives. It is easier to achieve your objectives when you have the right types of jobs filled with the right types of people supporting your efforts. This is called strategic staffing or sometimes, competency modeling. It is hiring the best candidates into the types of positions you need to accomplish your goals. Staffing must be mission-specific and goal-oriented.

What types of sales positions do you need to fill to become a value added sales organization?

What additional resources (equipment, processes, services, etc.) do you need to build this value added sales culture?

What To Look for in a Salesperson

If you started reading at this point, go back and read everything from the beginning of this chapter; otherwise, this section will make little sense. Do you know what to look for in a salesperson? You have identified the type of sales position for which you are staffing strategically. Now, you want someone that meets the demands of the job—someone that is more than a warm body in a hot territory.

Whom should you hire? You want someone that meets the demands and challenges of a sales position in a value added sales culture. That person should embrace the attitudes and beliefs, possess the attributes and values, and have the competencies, skills and knowledge to perform well in your sales culture and help you achieve your goals. If the candidate does not add value to your sales team, he or she is slowing you down and inhibiting your reaching your goals. You will not achieve your goals and the company's mission with a warm body in a hot territory.

The reason there are no perfect salespeople is that there are no perfect managers. Perfection is elusive.

Attitudes

Here are some of the attitudes and beliefs your sales candidates should possess. Can you teach them these attitudes and beliefs? Yes, but it is easier to begin with someone who already possesses these attitudes and beliefs. Whom should you hire? First, you must choose salespeople that embrace the attitudes, beliefs, and values that define your culture. For example, if you are staffing for a value added sales culture you want your candidates to share these attitudes:

"The sale is always about the customer." This attitude means that the salesperson realizes the importance of a customer-focused sales approach.

"I pursue excellence in all that I do." This attitude describes a salesperson that is positively addicted to doing things well.

"Value-Added Selling is a team sport." This attitude means the salesperson is willing to subordinate his or her ego for the greater good of serving customers and working harmoniously with others.

"If it is to be, it is up to me." This attitude describes a sales-person who takes the initiative to create results—someone who possesses an internal kick starter.

"Trust is the currency of great relationships." This attitude means that the salesperson values integrity in his or her relation-ships with others. People want to do business with those whom they trust.

Abilities, skills, and knowledge

Examine the candidate's raw material—natural talents and acquired skills. You may even want to test for this information. Ask these questions:

- Is this candidate qualified for the job?
- Does the candidate have what it takes to perform this job effectively?
- If not, can we teach this salesperson what he or she needs to learn?
- Can he or she learn it?
- How is the candidate's technical knowledge?
- Do we have the time, resources, and inclination to develop this candidate?

Sales Force Competencies

Value added salespeople draw from a wellspring of knowledge (about sales, their industry, their customers, their competition, and their companies) to master the skills of their profession. These are skill areas for establishing sales force competencies:

- Strategic thinking and planning
- Organizing
- Recognizing viable sales opportunities
- Initiating contact (prospecting)
- Identifying buyer's needs

- Brainstorming solutions
- Persuading buyers to choose one's alternatives
- Negotiating contracts
- Resolving objections
- Supply chain monitoring and logistics support
- Assuring customer satisfaction
- Re-creating value after the sale
- Value reinforcement
- Leveraging business relationships

The best executive is the one who has sense enough to pick good men (people) to do what he wants done, and self-restraint enough to keep from meddling with them while they do it. (Theodore Roosevelt)

Personal attributes

Companies invest significant time and money testing salespeople. These personal characteristics reflect the ideal balance of task and people orientation.

Ego-strength—this represents a sense of competence that emanates from a healthy self-esteem. The salesperson has a good sense of oneself—strengths and weaknesses. Because of high ego-strength, the salesperson has the courage to make the tough calls, the assertiveness to meet new people, the confidence to be persuasive, and the ability to work independently. His or her inner strength resonates in determination, perseverance, and resilience. Because he or she is comfortable in his or her own skin, this salesperson is willing to risk and explore possibilities. This fuels creativity.

Drive—this is the energy that makes it happen. You see this motivation in the salesperson's ambition, will-to-succeed, and initiative. The salesperson assumes full ownership for his or her success and results. He or she exudes optimism and a positive sense-of-control over one's destiny. This positive sense-of-control extends to the salesperson's environment and self-control of emotions. This salesperson has a positive addiction to excellence and takes pride in his or her efforts. He or she displays a conscientious, take-charge attitude.

Empathy—this is the ability to define the world in terms bigger than oneself. A salesperson that scores high on this dimension is able to view things from another's perspective and will ask questions and listen attentively. This salesperson will subordinate his or her ego for the greater good of serving. This is the consummate team player. Whether it is working together with fellow employees, peers or customers, this salesperson realizes that we is greater than me. High-empathy salespeople are perceptive. They understand their impact on others. They are cognizant of the subtleties in relationships. They define value and success in customer terms. Empathy also provides balance for aggressive salespeople.

Values

Values lie at the core of motivated behavior. In addition to the values inherent in your company's culture, these are some of the things your salespeople must value:

- Integrity
- Autonomy
- Teamwork
- Relationships
- Initiative
- Success

Where To Find Candidates

Everywhere. This is where I am really going to bend your comfort zone. There are some realities that you must accept if you plan to find and attract these candidates. First, some people are naturally better at sales—the phenoms. They bring to the table a host of personal skills and attributes that we see in great salespeople. These people may be in your company or in the general population.

Second, many of these people currently are not employed in sales. They may be teachers, technicians, customer service reps, counselors, hairdressers, construction workers, truck drivers, and waiters. They are in every profession. If you limit your search only to people currently employed as salespeople, you are ignoring the eighty percent that could potentially sell circles around the twenty percent employed as salespeople. It is like saying the best political candidates are already in politics. Research indicates more people in the general population stand a greater chance for success in sales than half of those who currently work in sales.

Third, your competition for great salespeople is not your industry. It is the entire economy. Any company that hires salespeople is your competition. Most product knowledge is teachable; no one is born knowing things about a product or industry. It is a grave mistake and the height of arrogance to believe that your industry has a monopoly on talent. Some industries are so incestuous that they trade only on each others' salespeople. Things are not different in your industry. Most people are not born into an industry. They gravitate.

Fourth, you must be proactive in your search. If you wait for the need to surface, you will feel great urgency to hire a body. This is one of the ironies of sales management. You expect your salespeople to prospect continuously for new business, but you fail to practice this sage advice yourself. Your selection process goes a lot smoother when you have a file drawer full of good résumés from viable candidates. You will make better strategic hiring decisions.

Customer relationships are too important to squander with mediocre performers. It sends the wrong message to the customer. You are saying, "We're sending you a mediocre salesperson, because that's how we value your business." As sales manager, your job is to achieve organizational objectives with the resources you have available. When you hire the best people you can find for the job, it increases the probability that you will succeed in your position. Coaching is always easier when you have the right talent on staff. Hire strategically.

Being proactive in recruiting means never having to say you're sorry for hiring a warm body for a hot territory.

Surround yourself with salespeople that embrace your company's mission, share its cultural beliefs and attitudes, have the raw talent to perform the job, and the personal attributes instrumental to their success. Look everywhere. They are out there, in and out of sales.

Sample Interview Questions

When interviewing candidates for a value added sales culture, ask these questions to give you insight into this person:

- What do you expect from management? (autonomy)
- How often do you prospect and why? (self-starter)
- What is the first thing you do in the morning when you arrive at the office? (organized)
- How do you set priorities? (planning ability)
- What do customers look for in salespeople? (this is a peek inside the candidate's head)
- What techniques do you use to keep yourself on a *sales high*? (self-reliance)

- How does selling fit into your career path? (long-term thinker)
- What role has luck played in your life? (lucky or good)
- How do you get new product ideas? (creative)
- Describe your most successful sale. (insightful)
- How did you deal with your greatest defeat? (resilience)
- What motivates you to win? (introspective)
- How do you prepare for a sales call? (organized)
- What selling skill has helped you the most? (thoughtful)
- Which type of customer is the hardest for you to sell? (insightful)
- How soon after the sale do you contact your customers? (follow-through)

Candidate Evaluation

These are some questions to ask yourself behind the scenes about the candidate you are evaluating:

- Did the references check out?
- Does the résumé reflect stability?
- Are all time gaps accounted for on the résumé?
- Does the candidate have a record of success?
- Did candidate use the word "honest" in the interview to describe successful salespeople or what buyers want?
- Did the candidate show initiative in the interview?
- Did the candidate ask for a tour, request literature, or ask when he could start?
- Did his language indicate he or she was in control of his or her destiny?
- Did the candidate blame the economy, a poor product line, or a lack of support for his failure?

- Did the candidate discuss the importance of the customer to his or her long-term success?
- Did she appear to be customer-oriented versus product-oriented?
- Were her questions thorough?
- Was the candidate's résumé thorough?
- Did the candidate contact me after the interview?
- Did I get the impression that this candidate is proactive or reactive?
- Did the candidate listen well?
- Was his eye contact steady?
- Were her nonverbals open?
- Were her questions thought-inspiring?
- Was the candidate prepared for the interview?
- Does the candidate have a method for keeping himself organized?
- Did this candidate ask for the job?
- Would this candidate bring value to our sales team?

Summary

You want more than a warm body in a hot territory. To select the right person, study the job through the prism of your objectives—departmental and company. Strategically staff your sales force with the type of salespeople that will help you accomplish your mission. Hire people that embrace the attitudes and beliefs of value added salespeople. Surround yourself with salespeople that add value to your sales team. These salespeople are everywhere. One great sales management myth is that salespeople exist only in the ranks of current salespeople or in the industry in which you currently work. If you rely solely on industry talent, you deprive yourself of a larger pool of successful candidates. Be proactive in your search. The best time to look for salespeople is before you need them.

To get the most value from this chapter, write your action steps for using these ideas.

_____

_____

_____

CHAPTER THREE:
SETTING SALES OBJECTIVES

Consider this:

- 61% of workers have clear performance objectives.
- 39% of salespeople do not have written sales objectives.
- 26% of workers said their managers regularly coach them on these objectives.

You have recruited the right people to support your mission to become a value added sales culture. Your company has a vision that translates into objectives for you and your salespeople. Your sales force executes tactically your strategic objectives.

This chapter is about sales management infrastructure Dynamic Number Two: How to establish comprehensive, mission-focused, highly motivating sales objectives that encourage your salespeople to stretch, not snap.

Goals represent many things. They are directional pursuits that guide us to an end point. A goal is a commitment to a certain course of action. It is a habit or a way of life. Goals are important because they add purpose and direction to your life. Goals inspire and ensure that you engage in high-priority activities that produce greater results. Goals help you to become more time efficient. They ensure you live balanced lives. Goals give you feedback on your daily efforts. When you achieve your goals, you know you are on the right track in life—that your work and personal habits support your calling in life. Salespeople with goals are more likely to help you get to where you want to be.

Goals without plans are wishes. When you plan your vacation, you usually begin with the end in mind. You select a destination and plan how to get there. You do not wish your way to the goal; you plan your way to the goal—the vacation spot. Coach your salespeople to plan their journeys to their successes.

Set SMART Goals

Observe these criteria to set "SMART" goals:

Specific—specify exactly what you want your salespeople to accomplish. If you want to increase customer retention, give your salespeople a target to hit. For example, if you currently operate at 85% customer retention, your goal may be to increase customer retention to 90%. Follow up with why this goal is important.

Less than one in four salespeople has a detailed plan-of-attack for their number one account.

Measurable—set goals that are measurable. This gives your salespeople feedback on their performance. Saying that you want more satisfied customers is okay if you can measure customer satisfaction. Measurability tells you that you have selected behavioral goals. These are goals over which salespeople have more control.

Aggressive—these goals are challenging and the most delicate to balance. You want goals that encourage salespeople to reach beyond their immediate grasp—not too high. Goals that are set too high de-motivate because they frustrate. Goals that are set too low de-motivate because they lack challenge.

Realistic—can your salespeople actually achieve what you are asking them to achieve with the resources they have available? People can walk on the moon, as we have already demonstrated, but few people have the resources to make this happen. Asking your sales force to raise prices by 15% in a tough economy could be more hopeful thinking on your part than reality for most salespeople. It may not be impossible, but you may want to revisit your discussion on that objective.

Time-sensitive—always have a time element embedded in your goals so that your salespeople know this is not an open-ended project. It is amazing how much work really gets done close to the deadline. Think about how much work you get done the day before vacation. Knowing when something must be accomplished helps your sales force plan more effectively by setting better priorities.

Setting Sales Objectives

The sales goals you set for and with your salespeople will be the performance standards that you use to give them feedback on their efforts. Measure what you will feed back.

Inspect what you expect; expect what you can inspect.

These tips help you set positive and motivating sales goals.

Time horizon—have short-term and long-term goals. Short-term goals give immediate feedback along the path to long-term goals. If the goals you set are measured too far in the future, your salespeople will have less information about their performance. When I flew airplanes, I designed a flight plan with a final destination in mind. I planned checkpoints along the flight path to check on myself. These checkpoints—every ten minutes—kept me on course. Short-term goals are checkpoints for your salespeople along their journeys. Annual sales quotas are fine as long as your salespeople get monthly feedback on how well they are performing toward this long-term goal.

Reinforcers—use a variety of reinforcement for achieving goals. Money is only one way to reinforce sales behavior. Praise, recognition, the opportunity to work on more challenging projects, training, and incentive trips are a few examples of things that also work well. And here is a key point for motivational reinforcement: The shorter the link between the behavior and the reinforcer, the more powerful the reinforcer. This is why short-term goals support long-term goals.

Perceived barriers—barrier analysis prevents barrier paralysis. Once you set sales objectives, ask your salespeople this question, "Do you see any reason why you cannot achieve these objectives?" The key dynamic you are working with is the salesperson's perception. Perception is subjective reality. What your salespeople perceive, they believe. Their perceived barriers are real to them. Identifying perceived barriers early in the goal-setting process and discussing potential solutions will help eliminate the excuses you hear in the long term.

Two-thirds of employees say they could contribute more value to their companies if they were involved in the decisions that affect them.

Performance and productivity goals—productivity goals tell your salespeople how much you want them to *accomplish*. Gross sales, profitability, and product-mix quotas fit this description. Performance goals tell your salespeople how you want them to *act* or behave. Making a certain number of calls per day, attending twenty hours of training per year, and visiting the office weekly are examples of performance goals. These activity-based goals are motivating because salespeople have greater control over their behavior than they do over results. Your salespeople may not be able to control fully the outcome of their efforts but they can control what they put into it. If you set performance goals (calls made) against a backdrop of productivity goals (sales made), the former should lead to the latter. For example, twenty sales calls per week (performance goal) will lead to achieving sales quota (productivity goal). Granted, your salespeople are not paid to make calls, they are paid to make sales, but making calls will lead to making sales.

Involvement—when your salespeople are involved in the goal-setting process, they are more committed to the goals. Involvement lowers resistance to change while building commitment. Research shows that salespeople who set their own goals will set higher goals than the manager would have set. You may find yourself lowering the goals that your salespeople set.

Product mix—goal-setting is a great opportunity for you to secure a broader product mix. Let salespeople know that you expect them to sell across the entire product line. Cross-selling or expanding the breadth of products sold strengthens ties with customers while increasing sales and profitability. Selling more things to an existing account is cost-effective for your company and your customer. Establish product mix targets, and give your salespeople feedback on their performance.

Offensive selling—this is pursuing new business. Advise your salespeople that you want them to spend a specified amount of time calling on new business and that you expect them to bring in a certain amount of new business each year. Offensive selling goals include both performance and productivity measurements. You want them to keep their pipelines full at all times, but not at the expense of our next topic.

Defensive selling—this is protecting and growing existing business. Calling standards for the amount of time spent with existing customers is a performance goal: Tell your salespeople that you want them to spend 80% of their time with existing customers. Customer retention and satisfaction numbers are productivity goals. Give them a retention target to shoot for. For example, you may challenge them to raise customer retention to 90%. Using offensive selling and defensive selling objectives provides balance in your sales goals and satisfies the demands of the value added sales culture.

Coach your salespeople to invest 80% of their sales time with existing customers and 20% with prospects.

Self-development—do you want your salespeople to continue to learn and grow? Set objectives for them to attend a certain amount of training every year. This is a performance goal. One Fortune 100 company requires their salespeople to attend forty hours of professional training every year. These performance goals will eventually lead to greater productivity. Other self-development goals may include reading books on selling, negotiating or time management. Becoming proficient with technology is a growth and development goal.

Internal selling—this is building relationships with peers on the inside. Your sales team must focus inward to build stronger ties with their internal customers. Value-Added Selling is a team sport. Inviting internal team members to make calls with salespeople builds relationships while exposing internal team members to the rigors of selling. Having your salespeople work in the warehouse or in the office gives them a different view of what happens on the inside. This builds empathy and understanding.

Profit and volume—most sales forces have a sales volume quota; few have a profit margin quota. For you to become a true value added sales organization, you must teach your staff to view sales through the profit prism. Not only will they become better salespeople, they will become better businesspeople. It teaches your staff to think strategically. When a salesperson must meet profit goals, they view discounting differently.

How can you set better goals for your sales force?

_____

_____

_____

Summary

Goals motivate and de-motivate. Goals behavioralize your expectations. Too much or too little challenge in goal setting is self-defeating. Goals add purpose to your efforts. They tell you if you are on track vis-à-vis the company mission. Goals are sign posts along your success journey. To get the most from your salespeople, set SMART goals, and involve them in the goal-setting process. Establish performance goals and productivity goals. When setting goals, focus on cold calling, repeat calling, product mix, profit and volume. Having goals that encourage salespeople to attend training and to grow professionally support your efforts at becoming a value added sales culture.

To get the most value from this chapter, write your action steps for using these ideas.

_____

_____

_____

CHAPTER FOUR:
TRAINING AND DEVELOPMENT

Consider this:

- The average salesperson receives one week of training per year.

- The average salesperson receives more product training than selling skills training.

- In a widely publicized study, Motorola University reports receiving a 33-to-1 return on training dollars spent on increased worker productivity.

Training is how you prepare your salespeople to perform their jobs. You have a mission, handed down to you by your management. Your objectives reflect this mission. You have analyzed the sales jobs that will support this mission, recruited salespeople who bring value to this job, and challenged them with sales objectives that tactically support your strategy. Now, it is time to prepare them for the challenge via training.

This chapter is about sales management infrastructure Dynamic Number Three: Preparing your salespeople for the sales challenges they face. You would not send an army into battle, an athletic team into competition, or an orchestra to a concert without preparing them for their challenge. Why would you send salespeople into the field without training them? This chapter is about preparing your salespeople by creating a learning culture in your company—a culture where your salespeople view learning as an ongoing process, not an isolated event.

Professionals prepare. Can you imagine someone wanting to become an airline pilot without going through the training? Would you hire someone to operate a lift truck and not provide them with some training? Have you been trained as a manager? If not then you really need this book!

During times of peace the most important task of any military is to prepare for war…the purpose of all training is to develop forces that can win in combat.
(Warfighting: The U.S. Marine Corps Book of Strategy)

Your salespeople are the mouthpieces of your organization. They broadcast all kinds of messages to customers. Are you curious what they are saying? Training protects your image by shaping the way your sales force takes this message to the customer. It is perfecting the message and preparing the messenger.

Your mission is to train for results. The driving question behind your train-for-results efforts should be: What do your salespeople need to know and be able to do to execute successfully the duties and responsibilities of their jobs? This helps you accomplish your goals and the company's mission.

Let's begin with a definition of terms. Training is preparing your employees for the jobs they are doing today. Development, which is often used in conjunction with training, means preparing your people for tomorrow—it is mind-stretching. Whereas training has an element of immediacy attached to it, development spans the future.

A learning culture is an environment where employees view learning, growth and development as natural. They embrace the concept of ongoing development and seek learning opportunities.

The goal is to make learning and growth cultural. Is learning cultural in your company now?

If your management made a decision to cease all research and development of new products, services and technologies, what would happen to your position in the marketplace? When I ask this question in seminars, I hear a variety of responses, but they all sound like, "We would lose our competitive advantage, and I would polish my résumé." Employees know when a company stops growing and developing new ideas, it is doomed for failure. The follow-up question I ask is, "When was the last time you invested in your personal research and development?" This is more of a rhetorical question that raises eyebrows. The product over which you and your employees have the most control is yourselves and the value you and they bring to the table. You and your salespeople are a brand that needs ongoing development. This happens in a learning culture.

The Needs Analysis

Whether we use this term in sales or in management, I am reminded of the adage, "Measure twice, and cut once." Some companies decide they need to spend money on training and other companies decide they need to invest in training. I get calls from both. Companies that want to spend money on training will say, "We haven't spent anything on our salespeople in a while, what can you do?" They want an event for their employees. This is typically more motivational or inspirational. Companies that want to invest in training for their employees call with a specific agenda in mind, based on an analysis they have conducted. Their goals are more specific.

To maximize your sales training dollars, achieve your departmental objectives, and accomplish your company's mission, you must conduct a needs analysis to identify the gaps that exist between your sales force's abilities and the demands of the job. What do your salespeople need to meet the demands of their jobs? What do they need to be able to do, and where are they now? This gap analysis is a foundation for your training and development efforts. Before you spend money on programs, be clear on your expectations and your desired outcome for the training.

Assessing your group's needs is the important first step in the training and development process. These ideas will help you determine your training focus. If I were to design a training program based on your needs, I would ask these questions.

- Is it a training issue? Are you convinced that you have the right people in the job? Training is easy with the right salespeople and difficult with the wrong salespeople. If you have a square peg in a round hole, begin with a different peg! If it is a selection problem, training will have minimal impact. There is an old saying that goes something like this: "You can tell a mule that he is a race horse, feed him like a race horse, train him like a race horse, run him like a race horse, but at the end of the day, he is still a mule."

- Who is the target group? Do you really want everyone to go through the training or would it be better for part of the group to attend only some sessions. Is it a whole-group issue? What would it hurt if they all went through it anyway? The spin-off benefits of training yield other advantages such as increased morale.

- What are your behavioral objectives? What do you want to see the group do differently after the training that they are not doing right now? What behavioral changes in their selling would justify the time and money you will invest in training them? What do you ideally want versus what is a minimally acceptable outcome? Your training objectives should support your departmental goals of becoming a value added sales culture and your company's goal of accomplishing its mission.

- What objections do your salespeople hear? Analyzing customer objections focuses on the areas where your salespeople need the most help: combating price resistance; understanding customer needs; telling your story; resolving objections; etc.

- "What prevents you from performing at the level you feel you are capable of performing?" This is one of the better questions to ask your salespeople about the obstacles they face. Build training around these issues. This is similar to the principle that appeared in the chapter on goal setting—barrier analysis prevents barrier paralysis. Eliminating perceived barriers eliminates excuses.

- What are my logistics concerns? Where will I train? When will I do it? How long should it last? Do I use internal or external resources? Is a morning or afternoon session preferable? What budget range am I working with?

Skills Development Questionnaire

Explore these topic areas with salespeople before designing training programs. You want their input, suggestions and feedback on where they think they need the most help. This, coupled with an in-field analysis of their sales behavior, give you in-depth understanding of your training needs. These topics should run parallel to your list of job competencies that we reviewed in the chapter on recruiting.

Instructions to salespeople: Please indicate your interest in learning more about the following topics by selecting the six that are most important to you. Label them 1 through 6, with 1 being the most important:

- Call preparation
- Building rapport with customers
- Probing and qualifying customer needs
- Presenting your value added solution
- Closing the sale
- Resolving objections
- Handling price resistance
- Follow-up strategies
- Selecting target accounts
- Gaining maximum account penetration
- Account classification
- Allocating sales time to accounts
- Account planning and strategy
- People reading
- Dealing with different types of customers
- Becoming a better listener
- Nonverbal communication
- Building stronger relationships with customers
- Setting priorities
- Maintaining your focus
- Becoming more efficient
- Blasting out of comfort zones
- Handling rejection
- Staying motivated
- Negotiating with customers
- Presenting to groups
- Selling to high-level decision makers
- Increasing customer loyalty and retention

Who Should Do the Training?

Where should you go for the training? Do you want to look inside or outside of your organization? If you have a training department, can they handle the assignment? If you go outside the organization, what will your training department say about that? The fundamental issue is whether you have the expertise and resources to do this training yourself or must you solicit the help from someone else? Is your time best spent designing this type of program or are you better off delegating or hiring someone to do this for you?

Going outside for expertise in a specific area gives you the most current information available on the topic. Investing in this type of training sends a message of support to your salespeople as well. Companies spend money on people they care about. They invest money in people they believe in. Regardless of the training method you choose, as sales coach, you are still responsible for follow-up. Training is about the *acquisition* of knowledge and skills; coaching is about the *application* of this knowledge and skills. Your follow-up can yield a four-fold return on money invested! That's what the research shows: Managers who follow up on training to coach and reinforce it get four times the results as managers who fail to follow up. If it is to be, it is up to you. You are responsible. You are accountable. It is all about your performing your job as coach.

Adult Learning Theory

Your knowledge of adult learning theory will help you present material in your sales meetings and training sessions that is interesting and helpful to the group. Remember these tips about adult learning when designing and delivering your information. Adults learn best when:

- Training reflects real-life situations they experience.

- They understand the importance of the material.
- They can use current knowledge (frame-of-reference) to process new information.
- They are able to integrate new information into what they already know.
- They can use their real life experiences to understand the material.
- They are involved physically and mentally.
- They are ready to learn: They want, need, and appreciate the training.
- They are guided versus graded.
- They are in an informal environment.

Meeting Tips

These ideas will help you conduct more effective training meetings.

Before meeting

- Determine your itinerary. Prepare a written agenda.
- Send a memo detailing times and emphasize timeliness versus tardiness.
- Do a cost versus return to determine if the meeting is worthwhile.
- Determine if everyone needs to be there for the whole meeting.
- Know what you expect each person to contribute.
- Choose the most appropriate time and location. Allow adequate time to accomplish the objective of your meeting, but never fail to set a time limit for all meetings.
- Start and end on time.

Conducting meetings

- State ground rules.

- Make it exciting through interaction and participation.
- Present one training topic per meeting.
- Utilize a participant/leader for selling techniques.
- Keep the pace appropriate to the learning objective.
- Present important things first.
- End with a call-to-action statement: Challenge the group to use what they have learned. Ask for a commitment.
- Indicate you will follow up on their commitment.
- Share the floor unless it is an information-only meeting and you are the one giving the information.
- Avoid getting caught in a conversational cross-fire between participants.
- Be assertive enough to wrap up each topic on time.
- Steer the discussion back on track as soon as it veers.
- Place value on the contributions of others; give constructive recognition. It promotes team spirit.
- Be clear and concise in your remarks.
- Use meeting follow-up sheets for assignments.
- Be as organized as possible.
- Use visual aids if they will clarify what you are saying.
- Be aware of your distracting mannerisms. Watch a videotape of yourself and expect a few surprises!
- Close the meeting on a positive note. Mention their progress and the worthy contributions.
- If needed, arrange follow-up meetings with individuals for further clarification of their duties or meet on-the-spot before you leave the meeting.
- Note follow-up dates on your calendar.

Group Dynamics

- To get a group going, use direct questions.

- To prevent monopoly by one or two participants, ask non-participants for opinions.
- To stop everyone from talking at once, ask specific participants directed questions.
- To stop the group from lingering too long on one subject and prevent the group from losing momentum, use closed-ended questions.
- To prevent group from rambling, use closed-ended questions or summarizing statements.
- To stop group from polarizing (by age, sex, experience, responsibility), return to the last point of group consensus; seek other points of consensus; call attention to what is happening; and recap your objectives for the meeting.
- To encourage expression if the group is reluctant to discuss issues or carry out exercises, use questioning to determine cause of problem. Use benefit statements to regain commitment.
- Neutralize abrasive questions from participants by reframing or restating their comments as questions.

Sales Meeting Format Model

This three-step meeting model will help you organize your training material and present with high-impact.

Introduction: "Tell 'em what you are gonna tell 'em!"
- Welcome the group and announce the topic.
- Expose the need for this training topic. Tell the group *why* the training is timely.
- Promise benefits for learning the skill.
- State the behavioral objectives and the anticipated training outcome.

Body: "Tell 'em!"
- Explain the concept and discuss it with questions and answers.
- Demonstrate the skill.
- Encourage group participation: paper and pencil, discussion, or role play.

Close: "Tell 'em what you told 'em!"
- Recap the session.
- Call for action.
- Assign follow-up tasks.

The Play Book

Good coaches prepare playbooks for their teams. It is the team's bible. It provides them with everything they need to know to excel in their positions. Use the play-book concept for your sales team. Design a success manual for your salespeople. This compendium of vital information guides your salespeople through their initial phases of training and adapting to the job. It serves as a reference manual as they grow in experience. Those who use this concept will notice that it cuts the learning curve for new hires, as they seize more opportunities quicker. In this manual, behavioralize your expectations and tell salespeople how to execute the job successfully. Include these topics in this binder:

Product knowledge—why should someone want to buy your products? In this section, provide your salespeople with the product knowledge they need to answer this question. Detail the product's operational features and application benefits. List all packaging options. Explain your pricing structure.

Company information—why should someone want to do business with your company? In this section, provide information on your company's policies, procedures, and value added. You could include a historical perspective of your company to give your sales team some roots to take to the field with them. Make them feel like they are part of the team.

Market information—what do your salespeople need to know about the market? Eighty-two percent of salespeople fail to differentiate themselves and their solution from the competition. What are the definable and defendable differences between you and the competition? You may be in the same industry as your competition, but you are not in the same business. Explain why.

The mark of a good salesperson is knowing what business to pursue; the mark of a great salesperson is knowing what business not to pursue.

Customers—with what type of customer do you want your salespeople to invest time? Clarifying this for your salespeople is the most immediate impact you can have on your sales force and their efforts to become a value added sales culture. Where do you want them to spend their sales time? When you answer this question clearly, you cut their learning time significantly, provided you know the type of business you want to pursue and the type of business you want to avoid. What is fundamentally good business for your company?

Letter writing—value added salespeople make it a habit to do what others consider to be a hassle. Most salespeople consider letter writing a hassle. Every sales letter is a marketing exposure. Offer some tips for better letter writing and include sales letters that cover every step of the sales process: getting appointments, sales call follow-up, proposals, and so on.

Case studies for success stories—this is one of the most powerful things you can do for your salespeople. Include six common case studies where your company faced obstacles and got the business anyway. Why did you get the business? What made the difference? How did you make the sales? New hires as well as experienced reps can learn from this.

Technology—what do your salespeople need to know about technology to successfully execute their jobs? This includes computers, sales force automation software, proprietary systems, phone systems, email operation, and personal data assistants.

Communication skills—listening and nonverbal communication play a major role in sales success. Communication skills build solid relationships with customers. Find articles on listening and persuasion to include in this section. You may even consider special topics like "gender speak."

Attitude—handling rejection and sustaining a positive mental attitude are key topics for salespeople. Few professions deal with rejection as often as salespeople must deal with it. Any resources you can provide your salespeople to help them maintain a positive focus will be helpful and appreciated.

Time management—how do you want your salespeople to spend their time? The two biggest time management challenges salespeople face are setting priorities and staying focused on these priorities. Explain to them how to set priorities and offer tips for remaining focused. You want them to use the same disciplined effort in running their territories as you use in running your sales department.

Objections—make a list of all the objections your salespeople hear. Survey your salespeople to build this list. Prepare a list of rebuttals for these objections. Offer creative ideas for handling resistance. Pay close attention to price objections since these present a special challenge. Salespeople appreciate this type of support. You are helping eliminate some of the barriers that interfere with their success.

The sales call—what type of sales call format do you want your salespeople to use? How should they prepare for a sales call? What type of sales objectives should they target? What questions do you want them to ask? What benefits should they stress? How do you want them to close? Provide a sample of this format in this section.

Summary

Training is the acquisition of skills to meet the immediate demands of the job. Development is mind-stretching—what people learn today for tomorrow. Both terms are used in the human resources field. A learning culture is an environment in which ongoing development is the rule, not the exception. Step One in training is the needs analysis. Here, you identify the gap that exists between where your salespeople are and where you want them to be. The decision to do the training yourself, or to hire someone else to do it, rests on your priorities and available resources. Prepare a play book for your salespeople with all the vital information they need to be successful in their jobs.

To get the most value from this chapter, write your action steps for using these ideas.

_____

_____

_____

CHAPTER FIVE: COMPENSATION

Consider this:

- 1/6 of salespeople are paid commission only.
- 2/3 of salespeople are paid a salary plus an incentive.
- 1/6 of salespeople are paid base only.
- 1/3 of the average sales compensation comes from incentives—bonus or commission.
- 2/3 of the average sales compensation comes from base salary.

You get what you pay for. Maybe. When it comes to compensation, are you getting as good as you are giving? Do your salespeople view their compensation as equitable? Is your compensation plan competitive? Does your plan motivate your salespeople? Do you offer unlimited earnings potential for your salespeople? These are just a few of the questions that keep sales executives awake at night.

You are building a value added sales culture: You have analyzed what you need in a salesperson, recruited to these needs, set challenging objectives, and trained your salespeople for success. Now, turn your attention to designing a compensation program to support your goal of becoming a value added sales culture.

On the surface, compensation sounds easy: Design a plan that compensates your sales force equitably, and everyone is happy. It is not that simple. Compensation is a complex aspect of sales management. Consultants specialize in this field. There are books dedicated to this topic. Seminars on compensation abound.

This chapter is about sales management infrastructure Dynamic Number Four: Compensating your salespeople equitably. It will pose more questions than provide more answers. My goal in this chapter is to challenge you with some fundamental ideas that cause you to re-think your compensation plan and the logic upon which it is built. This chapter is about building a compensation plan that helps you to create a value added sales culture.

What You Want To Reward and Reinforce

There are two fundamental compensation questions you must begin with: "What do we want to reward and reinforce?" and "Are we giving as good as we are getting, and are we getting as good as we are giving?" Your compensation plan begins with these questions. How you structure your plan depends on your sales objectives and company mission—in this case, to become a value added sales culture. You may want to reward and reinforce any or many of these things:

- Product mix
- Offensive selling—pursuing new business
- Defensive selling—increasing customer retention and growing business with customers
- Customer satisfaction
- Profitability
- Sales volume
- Pioneering a new brand or product
- Pioneering a new territory
- Cold calling
- Repeat calling
- Teamwork
- Professional growth and development

If your company's mission is to become known as the company that treats their customers with care and delivers great service and follow-through, your compensation plan must reinforce this objective. If your mission is to grow your business by expanding market share, you will compensate your salespeople differently.

Base, Bonus or Commission

So, what do you offer? A big base? Total commission? A mix of both with a bonus as a kicker? It depends on your sales management objectives. Each of these options has an upside and a downside.

Salary-only

This is easy to understand. It is out there for everyone to view. It removes some of the urgency that incentive salespeople feel. It may encourage more of a team attitude because one person does not really stand out money-wise. It also makes a volatile market easier to work in because one's compensation is more stable.

The downside of a salary-only program is that it removes some of the urgency salespeople feel to reach targets. This means money is a less powerful motivator. It increases your fixed selling costs because your base salaries are higher. A salary-only plan attracts salespeople who are stability oriented and may risk encouraging salespeople to land in a comfort zone. Salary-only plans tend to benefit mediocre performers and discourage high achievers.

Incentive plans

Commission-only plans encourage unlimited earnings and potential. These plans attract aggressive salespeople while repelling low-achieving salespeople. Salespeople who work in this environment feel they are paid what they are worth.

The downside is that in volatile markets salespeople can experience huge swings in their income. Management has less control over these salespeople, as these salespeople will view anything that detracts from their earnings time an imposition on their schedule. Commission plans also encourage a short-term, quick-hit mentality. Salespeople who are paid commission residuals on repeat business in an established territory may get comfortable with their income.

Bonus

Bonuses are paid in addition to a base salary and or commission. Bonuses allow you to reinforce more than sales quota, although bonuses are used for this also. Bonuses can be paid for short-term or long-term objectives. You can use them to reward qualitative sales objectives like: attending training, participating in trade shows, working weekends, increasing market share, raising customer satisfaction, and participating in industry seminars. Bonuses allow others in the company to participate in your plan.

How to Structure Your Plan

Structure your compensation to reflect the nature of the sales job. Is this a sales job that requires pioneering a brand or a territory? Does this job involve more cold calling or repeat calling?

If the sales position involves heavy cold calling, pay a higher percentage of commission versus bonus. Commission rewards high-level performance and offers a share of the sales gain.

Use bonuses for repeat business and specific objectives like increased customer satisfaction or retention, increased profitability, and product mix. Use bonuses for longer-term sales objectives like year-end performance goals.

If your sales position involves more offensive selling (cold calling) than defensive selling (repeat calling), use commission. If it involves more maintenance selling (defensive selling), use a higher percentage of a base salary with a smaller commission. You may choose to fill in the blanks with a bonus targeting some other sales objective. Most salespeople are paid some combination of a base salary plus a commission percentage and a bonus.

42% of companies cap the earnings of their salespeople; they fail to reward unlimited performance.

Few salespeople today are full-commissioned salespeople. These rugged individualists view their territories as their businesses and make many of the decisions that affect their territories. As you might suspect, new salespeople may not prefer to work as full-commissioned salespeople until they have established themselves.

Will you use a draw against commission? The draw gives the salesperson a small stipend to help with bills, but it generally does not offer enough compensation to live on. The incentive is to get off draw as soon as possible. When the salesperson's gross sales reach the breakeven point, the draw is paid out fully and the commission plan takes over.

Compensation Questions

These questions will help guide your efforts to fine tune your compensation plan:

- Does our current plan reward and reinforce sales behaviors that support our goals and mission? If not, why?
- Will we allow our salespeople to earn more money than management?
- Will we cap our salespeople's earnings? If so, why?
- If we cap the salesperson's earnings, how do we explain this to the sales force?

- Do we encourage a career sales mentality with our compensation package?
- Is individual or team compensation desirable for us?
- Other than money, what else can we offer to reward sales success?

When answering this last question, consider that people work for more than just the money. Money is only one way to reward behavior. One study of salespeople found that only one in three salespeople said they worked for the money. Two-thirds of the salespeople looked beyond the pay to the benefits, working conditions, management, career opportunities and autonomy.

Value-Added Selling Compensation Plan

If your goal is to build a value added sales culture, construct a pay plan that encourages your salespeople to sell offensively and defensively. Encourage your salespeople to fix one eye on present business and the other eye on growth opportunities. Profit plays an important role in establishing and rewarding value added sales objectives. Remember that Value-Added Selling is a team sport.

The following splits may reflect different sales objectives:

- Pay a base salary and commission for acquiring new business plus bonus for increasing customer retention, expanding product mix, and boosting profitability in one's territory.
- If it is an established territory, pay a higher base and use bonuses to reward specific objectives. If it is a newer territory, pay a lower base and a higher commission on new sales.
- Combining offensive and defensive sales objectives covers both ends of your business pipeline and encourages a growth mindset while protecting your existing base.

What is the fundamental thing we want to reinforce?

_____

_____

_____

How does our compensation plan compare with others in our industry?

_____

_____

_____

How does our compensation plan compare with others outside of our industry? Are we competitive across-the-board?

_____

_____

_____

In what ways should we consider modifying it to be more in line with our objectives and our mission?

_____

_____

_____

Summary

Compensation is a highly specialized topic. The fundamental question you must ask yourself is, "What do we want to reward and reinforce?" You must concern yourself with perceived equity issues with your sales force so that they feel they are getting as good as they are giving. By the same token, you want to get from your salespeople what you pay for. This chapter was about designing a specific type of sales compensation plan—a plan that encourages the growth of the value added sales culture.

To get the most value from this chapter, write your action steps for using these ideas.

_____

_____

_____

CHAPTER SIX: MOTIVATION

Consider this:

- 84% of employees say they are not performing to their potential.

- Money is not the universal motivator; it is not even a primary motivator. People do not work for money; they work for what the money buys them.

Coaches are motivators. Effective coaches know how to get the most out of their team. You are building a value added sales culture: You have analyzed what you need in a salesperson, re-cruited to these needs, set challenging objectives, designed a compensation program to support your goals, and trained your salespeople to perform at a high level. Now, turn your focus to motivating your salespeople.

This chapter is about sales management infrastructure Dynamic Number Five: Motivating your salespeople. It is a crash course in the study of sales behavior—a sales management MBA. Performance is a function of motivation and ability. This is good news for you as a manager because you can affect performance in two ways—how you motivate your salespeople and how much you teach them to increase their ability. In writing this chapter, I have drawn on my background in motivational psychology—why people do what they do.

Every act is the result of motivated behavior, pain or gain, fear or greed, and satisfaction or dissatisfaction. The more you know about motivation, the stronger your coaching technique.

When you understand motivation, you can predict behavior. Motivation is the energy that drives life. Understanding the principles of motivation equips you with what you need to know to fire up your group. If they are not fired up, you look bad. If they are fired up, they will walk across hot coals for you.

Motivation is an internal force that impels action. It comes from within the individual, which is important to consider when motivating others. Motivation is the result of a blend of internal and external forces acting on the individual. Stimulation is an external force that arouses action. The catalyst comes from the outside.

The best management lesson you will ever learn:
We motivate ourselves; others stimulate us.

At the core of motivated behavior are values. If you understand what others value, you can predict their behavior. People behave as they believe, and these beliefs are built on values that shape attitudes. Motivation theory deals with what people do. Values assessment deals with *why* they do what they do. Values shape beliefs and attitudes that influence behavior. Motivated behavior is a mix of values, beliefs, attitudes, needs, emotions and cognitions.

Rules of Motivation

Motivation is an internal process. It comes from within the person, an inside-out force. Understanding these rules of motivation will help you become a more effective sales coach.

- You cannot motivate another person. This sounds odd coming from someone in the motivation business. What you can do is create an environment where internal motivation to behave kicks in and the person does what you request. For example, you can lead a horse to water but not make it drink. If you ran the horse to the water, it will drink because it wants to drink. The motivation to drink (drive reduction) comes from inside the horse; you just changed its environment a little. This is why motivation is often referred to as the want-to.

- Everyone is motivated. Yes, it is true. Everyone is motivated; they are just motivated to do what they want to do or feel compelled to do. Even those people who appear un-motivated at work are motivated; they are just motivated to work less.

- People do things for their reasons, not anyone else's reasons. Motivation is a personal thing. When people do something, they do it for their reasons, and those reasons are rarely your reasons. In fact, they could not care less about your reasons for wanting them to do something.

- People rise or fall to their levels of expectations. These expectations may come from within themselves or from others. It has been said that people may not always get what they want, but they generally get what they expect. Over the years, management studies have shown that a manager's expectations influence the performance of his or her employees.

- Everyone has different levels of needs with individual capacities. The key to effective motivation is to identify what moves someone—psychological needs or physical needs—and figure out a way to give it to them on the job. Shaping the work environment to allow for need satisfaction yields the motivated behavior you desire from your employees. You are giving them the opportunity to work for and toward something they desire.

- Environments that offer challenge, demand creativity, and encourage growth are highly motivating. As a coach, your objective is to offer a sales climate that challenges and encourages your salespeople to meet these higher-level psychological needs on the job.

- Involvement and participation lower resistance to change and build commitment. As I stated in the section on establishing sales objectives, the more involved your salespeople are in the planning and decision process, the more committed they are to the process.

Intimidation brings compliance without commitment.

- Intimidation is a short-term motivator. The "kick-in-the-pants" model of moving people works from time-to-time as a catalyst to action, not as a sustainable form of motivation. It is tiring for the motivator and annoying to the motivated. When you use intimidation as a motivator, people only work hard enough to avoid the beating that you threaten.
- Money is not the universal motivator. If it were, there would be only one compensation plan in place and little need for other recognition and reinforcement programs. In one study, personal satisfaction, the opportunity to advance and gain respect and recognition ranked higher than money in employee preferences.

People are more highly motivated if these seven conditions are met:

- They feel they can achieve the desired behavior. For example, if you want your salespeople to cold call, they are more highly motivated to cold call if they feel they can execute the sales call successfully. Do they know how to make a cold call?

- They perceive few obstacles and feel competent in meeting these obstacles. This is why it is important to identify perceived barriers when setting goals. Again, barrier analysis prevents barrier paralysis.

- They feel challenged—not defeated. Too much challenge frustrates people and too little challenge bores them. Challenge should encourage people to stretch, not snap. Most salespeople who are in comfort zones feel under-challenged in their environments.

- Their behavior has a pay-off. "What's in it for me?" is the question most people ask themselves before deciding to act. And the payoff must be valuable to the individual. This is where your understanding of what motivates them pays off. Using this information, you can build high-value reinforcers into your rewards program.

- They are treated equitably. Employees ask themselves consciously and unconsciously, "Am I getting as good as I am giving?" In management psychology, this is called equity theory: People are motivated to perform if they feel that they get as good as they give. The question you must ask yourself is: Do their outcomes reflect their inputs? Do my salespeople feel that they are treated equitably with our compensation plan and reinforcement schedules?

- They have an internalized sense of mission. Commitment to a successful mission is a powerful motivator. Effective sales campaigns happen because the sales force embraces the company's mission and feels compelled to pursue it. I call this being a "maniac on a mission."

- They feel a sense of contribution and meaningfulness to their behavior. Mentally, they ask, "Is my job important and relevant?" People want to feel what they do contributes value to the organization. Everyone wants to feel useful and viable—that what they do matters in some fashion to someone.

How To Motivate Your Salespeople

Some activities are internally satisfying. Others depend on reinforcement from another source. As the coach, you will use this blend of internal and external motivators to create a highly motivating climate with the resources you have available.

Intrinsic motivation—the inner applause

People do things because something within the activity reinforces and satisfies them. The pleasure comes from "the doing" of the activity: e.g., creativity, challenge, joy, autonomy, control, a sense of accomplishment, and the desire to achieve and win.

When children play, they play because it is fun. It is intrinsically satisfying. When adults work in a profession that offers intrinsic satisfaction, they thrive. If your career is so pleasurable that you would do it even for free, you are working for the intrinsic satisfaction.

Intrinsic motivation is what gets you out of bed in the morning without an alarm clock; you cannot wait to get to work. If you work for the freedom of independent thought or creative exploration, you are intrinsically motivated. The pursuit of excellence is intrinsically motivating for some people. Intrinsic motivation comes from inside the activity, yet may still bring external rewards.

Extrinsic motivation—the cheers from the crowd

The pleasure or satisfaction comes from outside the task itself: e.g., money, titles, promotions, praise, and awards. You work for the rewards and the reinforcement that comes from outside the task. The payoff is external versus internal.

For example, if you work to buy things, you are motivated by acquisitiveness. If you perform at a high level because you like the recognition that comes from your achievement, you are motivated by status. You may be an incredibly competitive person and enjoy the game, the competition, and you feel good when you win. You are extrinsically motivated.

Leadership: The art of getting someone else to do something you want done because he wants to do it. (President Dwight D. Eisenhower)

Certain activities may contain elements of intrinsic and extrinsic motivation. Training is one of those areas. When you design sales training for your staff to help them perform at the top of their game, it is extrinsically rewarding—the payoff from learning new skills. It is intrinsically satisfying to learn new things and unleash one's creativity. It is extrinsically rewarding to receive the payoff—the pay, the praise, and the promotion.

As the coach of your sales team, your challenge is to find ways to tap into both forms of motivation. Shape the work environment so that the sales force feels the intrinsic satisfaction of working in a climate that taps into their creativity, autonomy, and pursuit of excellence and offers the external rewards of pay, praise, and recognition for a job well done.

When are you intrinsically and extrinsically motivated?

How can you make your job, as a sales manager and coach, more intrinsically and extrinsically satisfying?

_____

_____

_____

List ways to make your company's sales jobs more intrinsically and extrinsically satisfying:

_____

_____

_____

Motivational Things-To-Consider

Illustration 6-1 is a tool to help you understand the different levels of motivation. The goal is to create a motivational work climate by giving people the opportunity to meet all levels of needs on the job. Each person has different capacities and requirements at each level. Some people are more focused on one level than another. For example, you may be moved more by social needs, and your spouse may be more focused on basic needs. There is no right and there is no wrong. Some people meet higher level needs off the job. Why? Maybe they work in an environment that fails to offer this type of challenge. Meeting these levels of needs is a joint responsibility between managers and their employees. It is always management's responsibility to create a motivational climate, and it is always the employee's responsibility to create their own motivational climate.

Once a need level has been satisfied, it becomes less of a motivator and we are drawn to the next higher level of need. This answers the question many sales managers ask, "Why don't my salespeople work harder for the extra bonus?"

	Personal	Business	Motivators
Growth	Actualization Achievement Esteem Independence	Advancement Challenging work Titles Creative freedom	Growth and development Learning Job enrichment Control and autonomy Self-direction Participatory management
Social	Status Love Belongingness	Acceptance Part of the team Professional relationships Respect of peers and management	Praise and recognition Socialization Compliments Group activities
Basic	Safety Stability Status quo	Working conditions Benefits Money	Status quo Incentives Money, bonuses Favorable working conditions

Illustration 6-1: The Motivational Matrix™

Once the salesperson's need for money is satisfied, it becomes less important as a motivator; the urgency is gone. Again, this is why your job is to create a sales environment where all levels of needs can be satisfied on the job.

Coaches teach discipline, not administer it.

People who focus on higher-level needs tend to be more productive and experience higher levels of job satisfaction. This is because they are working for the intrinsic satisfaction of doing the job—they like it. Lower-level needs tend to be externally satisfied and upper-level needs tend to be internally satisfied. Lower-level needs rely more on extrinsic motivators; higher-level needs rely more on intrinsic motivators.

People have a burning desire to be better tomorrow than they are today. From the moment we are born, we aspire to grow, develop, and evolve. Our destiny is to grow and emerge. No one wakes up in the morning and plans to have a mediocre day. No salesperson begins the year with the most average goals in mind. Life itself is the expression of optimism. It is fundamental to the human spirit to want to grow and evolve and engage each day with positive anticipation. For you, the coach, your challenge is to tap into this spirit and to encourage your salespeople to grow on the job.

What can you do to help your salespeople grow, evolve, and emerge in their jobs?

Motivational Questions

The following list of questions is designed to help you understand the motivational profiles of your salespeople. Think of a salesperson who challenges you as a manager—someone whom you experience difficulty motivating. Ask these questions about this person and see if you more clearly understand this person:

- Is this a high or low-maintenance employee?
- Is this person motivated more from within or from the outside?
- If calling is a problem, why?
- What obstacles interfere with this person's success?
- Is this person more results or procedures-oriented?
- Is this employee more reactive or proactive?
- Regarding reinforcers, which appeal most to this person?
  - Praise and recognition
  - Autonomy
  - Stability
  - Independence/Teamwork
  - Money
  - Titles
  - Competition (within oneself or with other people)
  - The feeling of a job well done
  - Creative exploration
  - Opportunity for advancement
  - Ability to input

Reinforcement Theory

Up to this point, we have focused on the *what* of motivation—physiological and psychological needs. Reinforcement theory is another approach to motivation. It offers guidelines for increasing the odds that specific motivated behaviors will repeat themselves. Behaviorism is stimulus-response psychology. Behavior is maintained by its consequences. This is a tenet of behaviorism and a building block in this theory. You reinforce behavior by what you say and do and by what you fail to say and do. These are important points in reinforcement theory:

- Reinforcement theory deals with behavior—something observable and measurable. It focuses on what happens outside the person versus what happens inside the individual.

- Reinforcement theory states there must be a relationship between behavior and consequences whether it is reward or punishment. One study of 1,600 workers found that 52% of the workers said they would produce more on the job if they were held accountable for the results as well as the process of doing the job.

- The shorter the interval between reinforcement and behavior, the stronger the effect of the reinforcement. This is the logic behind compensation plans that pay more frequently than annually. Salespeople react more favorably to ongoing feedback that tells them where they are, relative to their goals.

- The quickest way to change behavior is to reinforce initially the effort, not the results. Because so many people suffer from performance anxiety, it is important to shape the behavior you desire because this behavior will bring you the results you desire long-term. Notice the emphasis on the word initially. After a while, the focus shifts to results.

- Use continuous reinforcement to change behavior. Reward or punish every repetition of a behavior to shape the end result you desire. When changing behavior, you may need to accept that better is good enough and that perfection is elusive.

- Once the behavior is in place, use intermittent reinforcement to sustain behavior. This is the logic behind slot machines. People stuff money in them because they never know when the next payoff will occur.
- To extinguish a behavior, ignore it. Your failure to respond to the (undesirable) behavior eventually discourages the person from exhibiting this behavior.

Motivation Summary

According to the cognitive theories of motivation, people ask themselves these three questions before deciding to engage in certain behaviors. This is done consciously or unconsciously.

- If I try, can I be successful? (Can I perform the required task successfully?)
- If I am successful, is there a payoff? (Is there a reward for my efforts?)
- Is the payoff worth it? (Does it have value to me?)

As a sales coach, you can have an impact on these questions and answers based on how you structure your sales culture. As you help salespeople learn the necessary skills, eliminate perceived barriers, and create meaningful payoffs for your salespeople, you are using positive mental programming to influence their cognitive conversations with themselves. Positive self-talk creates a motivational environment for most employees.

Questions To Ask About the Job

As sales coach, you can ask yourself these questions about the sales jobs you have created. You will notice that the focus of motivation shifts now from the person to the job. Ask your salespeople for their input on their jobs. These questions call attention to the needs, cognitions and emotions that employees experience and bring with them to the job:

- Is it fun? Is this job intrinsically satisfying to do? Do I enjoy doing this work?
- Is it challenging? Are the goals just right—not too high, not too low?
- Is it mine? Do I have the autonomy to put my finger-prints all over it? Can I input creatively and exert control over the job?
- Is it meaningful? Does the outcome of my effort matter? Does this job contribute value to my company and to the customer?
- Is it equitable? Am I getting as good as I am giving? Are my rewards commensurate with my efforts?
- Am I needed? Do I play a vital role on this team? Do I belong?
- Am I recognized? Do I get credit for a job well done? Do others see the value in my efforts?

Motivation Exercise

Think of a struggling salesperson or someone with whom you, as the sales coach, have struggled. Based on what you have read in this chapter, what motivates this salesperson?

_____

_____

_____

What has been your motivational approach with this person in the past?

_____

_____

_____

How should you approach this salesperson to change?

_____

_____

_____

What is there about the content of the job that you can change to create a more highly motivating job to create a value added sales culture?

_____

_____

_____

What is there about the context of the job that you can change to create a more highly motivating job to create a value added sales culture?

_____

_____

_____

Summary

Motivation comes from within the individual. It is the energy that impels action. It is the result of a blend of internal and external forces operating on the individual. As the sales coach, the best you can hope to accomplish is to create an environment in which the salesperson's internal motivation to achieve flourishes in your care. Everyone is motivated; they are motivated to do what is important to them, not necessarily what is important to you. When motivating your salespeople, consider their needs, cognitions and emotions. To create a more highly motivating environment for the salesperson, ask a number of questions about the job to ensure it meets multiple levels of needs.

To get the most value from this chapter, write your action steps for using these ideas.

_____

_____

_____

CHAPTER SEVEN: COACHING

Consider these facts:

- 32% of salespeople do not make joint calls with their sales managers.
- 27% of salespeople get no coaching from their sales managers.

You have built a value added sales culture, recruited the talent, set challenging value added sales objectives, trained your staff, compensated their value added sales performance, and motivated them. Now, turn your attention to yourself, the coach. This is a huge opportunity area. Other sales managers—your competitors—are failing to get maximum performance and leverage from their salespeople. Coaching is where you can gain ground on the competition. We talk about salespeople out-selling the competition; now we focus on your out-coaching the competition.

This chapter is about sales management infrastructure Dynamic Number Six: Coaching your salespeople to success. It is why you bought this book, but you had to read to get here. In this chapter we define coaching, review coaching attributes and behaviors, attitudes, rules and the how-to's of coaching.

As sales manager, coaching is your primary responsibility. The coach's hat is the number one hat you wear. Teams need strong leaders, and your role is to lead your team. Your team members never reach their full potential without strong coaching to lead them down the path of success. If your salespeople do not achieve their goals, you do not achieve your goals, and the company fails to achieve its mission. Get the point?

What Is Coaching?

Coaching is where the rubber meets the road. It is the nexus of management and leadership. Managers direct resources toward achieving organizational objectives. Leaders inspire people to act in ways they may not have acted on their own. Managers attend to the process; leaders attend to the people. Your prescription is: Manage the process, but lead your people. This is the role of the coach. Coaching is where theory gets applied and becomes reality.

A coach is a teacher, tutor, guide, motivator, and sometimes a friend. Coaches instruct, inspire, and inform. Coaches provide feedback and encourage growth. They are honest, proactive, empathic, observant, and knowledgeable.

Leadership is the art of accomplishing what the science of management says you can get done. (Colin Powell)

Who were the great coaches in history, and why were they great? Was it because of their winning record or because of the impact they had on their team members? Here is a little-known fact about management. As a sales coach for new salespeople—i.e. salespeople who are new to the profession—you will be the most influential person in this salesperson's career. That is an awesome responsibility.

How do you bring value as a coach to your sales force? How would your salespeople describe you as a coach? Would you make it to the Sales Coach Hall of Fame or the Hall of Shame?

Review the following checklist to assess your sales coaching habits:

- I make joint calls often with my salespeople.
- I am approachable to my salespeople.
- I provide ongoing feedback on their performance.
- I conduct ongoing training sessions for my salespeople.
- I constantly think of ways to motivate my salespeople.
- I recruit often to identify the best talent.
- I attend training to become a better sales manager.
- I clearly communicate our mission to the sales force.
- I equip my team with the best available resources to accomplish their mission.
- I seek ways to break down barriers with other departments in my company.
- I study how other great sales teams excel and share this knowledge with my team.
- My salespeople would say I am the best coach they have ever had.

How many of these statements describe you as a coach? Do you see room for growth in this area? You cannot expect your salespeople to work hard on their professional development if you are not working equally hard on your professional development.

In the following spaces, list some thoughts for how you can become a more effective sales coach:

_____

_____

_____

Selling Managers

This brings up another point. Do you have account responsibility? Are you a selling manager? Many sales managers have accounts for which they are still responsible. It is a bad idea, and I will tell you why. If you have customers to take care of, your salespeople suffer. You have less time to coach them. You are faced with a choice: Your top customer calls and needs your help at the same time your salesperson asks for help. Which call for help will you answer? The customer, of course. Who suffers? The salesperson, of course.

I have heard all the explanations for why it makes sense to have selling managers, but none of these explanations mitigates the damage done or missed opportunities from a lack of committed sales coaching. How many great player coaches exist in professional sports? How many great conductors sit down to play music with their orchestras during concerts?

One argument I often hear is that account responsibility keeps the coach close to customers. That's a bogus argument because if you are making joint calls, you are close anyway. Another argument I hear is that some accounts are too valuable for salespeople to handle. What does that say to your sales force about your trust for them? I worked with a client whose owner of the company kept for himself his company's largest account. His salespeople viewed his action as greed and a lack of faith in their ability. How motivated were they to perform for this owner? Another argument is that a company cannot afford a sales manager or their company culture does not fit the traditional sales management model. If that is true, you cannot expect salespeople to perform at their peak without the hands-on guidance that a dedicated sales coach provides. Something will suffer.

Why Salespeople Do Not Sell

As the sales coach, one of the most important questions you encounter is why salespeople fail to sell. These are some of the more common reasons I have seen over the years.

Objectives—this includes a lack of objectives, incomplete objectives, or sales objectives that are too high or too low.

Task clarity—this is where salespeople are unclear what they are supposed to do. For example, how much time should they spend calling on new prospects versus existing customers?

No feedback—some salespeople receive no feedback on their performance. Some sales managers dismiss this by saying, "My people know when they are not performing. I don't need to tell them." That is the mindset of a disconnected manager.

Ability—some salespeople lack the ability to do the job. Maybe this person is in the wrong type of sales job.

Knowledge—seventy-six percent of the value added in North America comes from knowledge-based activities, but there are still some salespeople who lack the knowledge to perform at their peak.

Motivation—the sales environment in which they work fails to tap into their internal motivation to succeed.

Why do your salespeople fail to sell?

_____

_____

_____

Why Salespeople Do Not Sell Value Added

If Value-Added Selling makes sense as a viable competitive sales strategy, why do salespeople fail to sell value added? Here is what I have noticed.

Lack of knowledge—no one has taught them how to sell value added. Maybe the problem is more fundamental than that. Do they know your company's value added? A simple exercise to fix this problem is to have your sales group make a list of all the value added that your company brings to the table. Record their responses on a flip chart and discuss them. Share with them your knowledge of the strategies and tactics of the Value Added Sales Process™.

Lack of confidence—do your salespeople believe your company is a value added supplier? Do they feel you are better than the competition? Eighty-two percent of salespeople fail to differentiate their solution from the competition. Can your salespeople differentiate your solution from the myriad competitors you face?

Fear—salespeople fear losing the business. Ironically, Value-Added Selling is supposed to help salespeople differentiate their solution, but some may fear they will lose the business by charging more for their solution.

Projection—salespeople who are price shoppers in their own lives find more price shoppers than their peers that do not shop price. The salesperson who complains most about your prices being too high is probably a price shopper in his or her own life.

Guilt—some salespeople fear buyers will think they are gouging if they charge higher prices than the competition. This ties into your salespeople not believing in your solution and your value added? If you sell a product your salespeople can use, ask your salespeople this question at your next sales meeting, "How many of you own and use our product?"

Mixed management signals—if you waiver or waffle in your commitment to creating the value added sales culture, you are responsible for your staff's failure to sell value added. For example, if you shift your focus away from Value-Added Selling to meet short-term sales objectives—volume or capacity quotas—you are doing long-term damage to your mission of becoming a value added organization.

Use these spaces to record your ideas on why your salespeople fail to sell value added.

_____

_____

_____

Sales Coaching Rules

After hiring, coaching salespeople is the critical job function for sales managers. Coaching is an excellent feedback mechanism for on-going training and development of salespeople. Research shows that coaching can be at least as effective a training medium as classroom learning. Yet ironically, this is often relegated to "filler" status for the manager. Managers promise, "I will do it when I get the chance." And of course, the opportunity rarely presents itself. This is an example of the sales manager's willingness to spend money on the sales force but not time. These coaching rules will help guide your sales management coaching efforts:

- If salespeople report directly to you, coaching is your number one job. Even if you have account responsibility, coaching your salespeople is still your primary job function. This is how you add value to your sales team.
- If you believe you are too busy to coach, reread rule number one. Imagine saying to your family, "I am too busy to spend time with you."
- If you believe that hiring experienced professionals relieves you from coaching, reread rule number one. Even Tiger Woods works with a golf coach. Are your salespeople better at their jobs than Tiger is at golf?
- You cannot coach from the locker room. You must be in the field with your reps to provide them with accurate

and meaningful direct feedback. How many professional sports team coaches sit in the locker room during a game and wait to give feedback until after the game? They understand the importance of being on the field with the team. Coaching from the field gives you the opportunity to provide feedback when it can still make a difference in the outcome of the game.

Don't be a desk jockey! Get out of the office and into the field with your salespeople.

- Coaching is for the salesperson's benefit. This is not the time for you to unload pent-up frustration with the sales force. Your objective in coaching is to guide your salespeople, provide corrective feedback, and inspire them to rise to the challenge. It is about them, not you.

- As I stated in the section on reinforcement theory, the quickest way to change behavior is to reinforce initially the effort, not the results. Profit follows performance, and performance follows effort. If salespeople put forth the effort you desire, they will create the results you want. They need your on-the-spot coaching to adjust their performance to work more effectively.

- You coach behavior and shape attitudes. You have greater control over your sales force's behavior than you do their attitudes. However, the more you coach their behavior, the greater the likelihood you can influence their attitudes. If you coach them to perform at a certain level, their attitudes will shift to fit their behavior. Cold calling is a good example. When the sales force realizes that cold calling is not as difficult as they had imagined, their attitudes will shift to parallel the calling behavior.

As the sales coach, you provide two kinds of feedback—quantitative and qualitative.

Quantitative feedback is data driven: This is how *much* salespeople achieve—the quantity of their efforts

- Sales-to-quota
- Number of calls made
- Closing ratio
- Sales profitability
- Product mix
- Customer retention
- Paperwork

Qualitative feedback is effort driven: This is how *well* salespeople perform—the quality of their efforts

- Quality of the sales call
- Product knowledge
- Internal and external relationships—team work
- Attitude
- How the salesperson spends his or her time
- Is the salesperson achieving his or her career goals?

Tips for Delivering Feedback and Coaching

Providing feedback is coaching your salespeople. Use these ideas for delivering feedback—positive and negative—when coaching your staff:

- Inspect what you expect. Since behavior is maintained by its consequences, joint calling and feedback are important. If your salespeople recognize that you are not following through on your commitment to inspect what you expect from them, they get sloppy on their calls and paperwork.

- Be specific with your feedback. It does not matter whether you are praising or delivering "corrective criticism", the salesperson must know exactly what he is doing right or wrong. Never leave the salesperson guessing about his behavior.

- Ignore the small stuff. Often, sales managers nit-pick. Focus on major critical issues that affect performance.

- Use a variety of reinforcers. Managers often assume that commission or bonus on a sale is reward enough. Praise and recognition are effective complements to money.

Listen like a coach, not a boss.

- Focus on behavior. Avoid vague criticisms and references to attitude. If your salesperson's attitude stinks, cite behavioral examples (e.g. cynical comments, tardiness, or frowning). It is easier for the salesperson to change his or her attitude when he or she understands which behaviors signal a negative attitude to others.

- Explain the feedback. If you are having a problem with something the salesperson does or does not do, tell him why it is an issue. Once he understands your rationale, he will be more open to change.

- Lend a helping hand. If possible and prudent, help the person change the behavior. Change is easier when someone offers assistance. This proves your sincerity.

- Use a sandwiching technique to deliver criticism. When you must deliver negative feedback, begin with something positive and then deliver the criticism, explaining why it is an issue. Conclude with something positive. This technique demonstrates your concern and awareness of the positive as well as the negative.

- Give three times the praise as criticism. This is the bare minimum. Five times the praise as criticism is even better. The objective is to reinforce (a lot) the behavior you desire. If you are like most managers, you are not doing this enough.

- Do it often. Ongoing dialog between the salesperson and manager is critical to your success also. Nothing you say in your annual performance reviews should be a surprise. If you have been doing your job all along, the salesperson has heard it before. Any surprise means you failed to deal with the behavior in the past. This is unfair to the salesperson.

- Make it routine. Joint calling and feedback sessions should not be punishment for failing to do one's job. When done properly, salespeople grow to respect and welcome their coach's input. This happens when managers joint call regularly with salespeople and expectations are set.

- Show empathy. Everyone gets nervous and a little defensive when the boss starts handing out criticism. Most people feel anxious when they are performing on stage. Be understanding of this reality; it demonstrates your humanity.

- Standardize your feedback. When joint calling, have a standard format for delivering your feedback. This helps salespeople know what to expect and on what they will be evaluated. Also, it keeps you focused on mission-critical behavior.

Coaching Effectiveness and Efficiency

As sales coach, you want your salespeople to become more effective and efficient. Efficiency is doing things the right way.

Effectiveness is doing the right things. Peter Drucker wrote, "There is nothing so useless as doing efficiently that which you shouldn't do at all." Working on their effectiveness is a focus issue. Are they working on the right stuff? Efficiency is finding the best way to do the right stuff. Attending to these areas will help you target ways for your sales force to become more effective and efficient.

Coaching without a core philosophy is performing random acts of supervision.

Sales calls—are they calling on the right type of customers to support your value added sales objectives, and do they know the most expeditious way to navigate the process?

Time management—do they fill their days with priorities that add value to their efforts and help move you closer to your goals? Are they working on the right stuff? Are they using all the technology at their fingertips to work efficiently?

Internal relationships and teamwork—how well do your salespeople relate with other team members in the organization? Do they build each other up or break each other down?

Self-development—are your salespeople growing? Do they continue to invest in their personal research and development?

Administrivia—how well do they complete their paperwork and meet the administrative demands of the job?

Knowledge base—do you periodically review what your salespeople know and target areas for their growth?

Coaching in a Value Added Sales Culture

Ostensibly, your reason for reading this book is to create a value added sales culture. In Chapter One, I introduced you to The Value Added Sales Process™ model. This cradle-to-grave sales model parallels the buyers' Critical Buying Path™. Salespeople who embrace the Value-Added Selling philosophy and follow this sales process engage in specific offensive and defensive selling strategies. These strategies guide their sales efforts. As the sales coach, you are responsible for directing your salespeople. The following strategic coaching questions will help you focus your salespeople on your mission to become a value added sales culture.

Are you chasing the right business?

This is the most immediate impact you can have as a sales coach—helping your salespeople understand the type of business you want them to pursue. Ask and answer this question with and for them: What is good business for our company? What kind of business do we want to pursue and what kind of business do we want to avoid?

Are you talking to all the right people?

Value added salespeople penetrate accounts thoroughly—top-down, bottom-up, and at every level in between. Coach your salespeople to penetrate at the highest levels in an account. This is where financial decisions are made. You must be willing to make joint calls with your salespeople on these High-Level Decision Makers (HLDMs). Sixty-eight percent of these HLDMs want to meet their high-level counterparts—that's you.

Do you really know how your customers think?

Value added salespeople are customer focused; they view their solutions through their customers' eyes. Coach your sales force to understand thoroughly the buyer's needs, wants and fears—both organizationally and individually.

What image have you created in the customer's mind?

Positioning is how your company reaches inside the customer's mind and carves out a piece of territory. Salespeople are part of this process. What image do you want your salespeople to project? Coach your salespeople to present an image that is consistent with your marketing efforts. For example, what good is it for your company to project an image of the value added supplier in your industry and then have your salespeople discount as if you were Wal-Mart?

How have you differentiated our solution?

In your next sales meeting, ask your salespeople to answer this question, "What are the definable and defendable differences between us and the competition?" Brace yourself for their lack of responsiveness. Most salespeople will fail to provide an acceptable response. Equip them with marketing information and competitive intelligence.

Can you present a compelling reason for buyers to choose our alternative?

What you are looking for here is how well your salespeople customize your solution, maximize your perceived value, and demonstrate your performance value. Study their style as well as their substance.

How painless is it for the customer to buy from us?

This is the shift point in Value-Added Selling from offensive to defensive selling. This transitional phase for the customer is filled with opportunities for your salespeople to offer logistics and hand-holding support. This includes how painless your company makes it for the customer to order your goods and services. It is not all on the salesperson to create transitional support.

How is your personal and professional relationship with the customer?

Salespeople struggle with this strategy. Most recognize the importance of relationships between buyers and sellers. Few would argue they are meaningless. The coaching point is that your salespeople must maintain enough professional distance so that they can make the tough decisions and the tough calls when it comes to customers.

Are you working as hard to keep the business as you did to get the business?

Some companies (and salespeople) treat prospects better than they treat customers. This selling strategy (Tinkering) compels salespeople to look for ways to recreate value for customers, especially once they have the business. Coaching your salespeople to "tinker" means keeping them out of comfort zones. You will coach them to continue to look for ways to get better for the customer.

Are we getting credit for all of the value added we bring to the customer?

This coaching question refers to the defensive selling strategy, Value Reinforcement. Few companies get the credit they deserve for the value they deliver. You get credit when you ask for it. Coach your salespeople to brag positively about the service you deliver and the extras your company offers customers.

Are we getting all the business we should be getting from this customer?

Managers are so concerned with new customers that they often forget the best source of new business is with existing customers. It takes less time and money to sell more products and services to existing customers than it does to sell to new customers. Coach your salespeople to expand the depth and breadth of products sold to their existing customers.

These coaching questions parallel the selling strategies from The Value Added Sales Process™ model. Asking these questions often, in your sales meetings and when making joint calls with salespeople, will focus your sales force on your mission of becoming a value added sales culture. In the last section of this book, I have included readings and discussion questions on these eleven strategies for you to use when coaching your salespeople. You can use these exercises one-on-one or as part of a training session or sales meeting.

When to Coach

Coaching is an all-the-time management style. It is ongoing and ubiquitous. You coach on-the-spot and behind-the-scene. Curbstone coaching sessions have been shown to be at least as effective for training salespeople as formalized classroom instruction. Weekly performance improvement sessions give you the opportunity to review with your struggling or new salespeople their performance and what they need to do to get to the next level and achieve their (and your) goals. Quarterly and annual performance reviews are the cornerstones of feedback. This is what everyone thinks of when you mention coaching. In reality, quarterly and annual reviews formalize what you have been saying and feeding back all along.

One question always surfaces at this point in our coaching seminars, "With whom should I spend my coaching time?" Should you spend your time with your top achievers or your struggling reps? The answer offends most people's sense of fairness. Struggling reps deserve the opportunity for corrective feedback and direction, but the greatest return on your coaching time invested will come from investing time with your top reps. This is not to say that you should ignore salespeople who are struggling; they deserve your time, attention and guidance. But it is your top performers who will give you the results you desire.

The Positive Coaching Environment

Salespeople must feel they are working in an environment of concern and trust—that you care about their performance and growth. Integrity, trust, confidence, concern, openness, respect, and firmness must be present in your coaching environment. Your people want coaches who are firm and fair. When they make mistakes, they want you to provide them with directive and constructive feedback. They want you to reinforce their efforts as well as their results. They want you to treat failure as feedback. When they fail, they want you to deal with them privately. When they succeed they want you to praise them in public. Equally important is your helping them to understand their successes as well as their failures. They want to know what to repeat and what to avoid in the future.

Joint Call Tips

Ideally, you should make joint calls with each salesperson monthly. Depending on the size of your sales force, this may or may not be feasible. About half of all sales managers make monthly sales calls with their salespeople. Use the following ideas when making joint calls with your salespeople to give them maximum feedback and take advantage of this opportunity.

Pre-call
- Meet early to discuss your plans for the day.
- Ask these pre-call questions before every sales call:
  "What do you want to accomplish on this call?"
  Is this an information-gathering or information-giving sales call? Is this sales call to build momentum, generate support, provide a demonstration for a product, or sell a specific application?
  "What action do you want from the customer at the end of the call?"
  This is the payoff question. It is what the salesperson asks for at the end of the sales call: a firm commitment to buy, a follow-up appointment, or credit information. The answer to this question is closing the sale.

During the call

- Remain silent. You are there to observe, not sell. It is the salesperson's show. Remember what Yogi said, "Much can be observed by just watching."

- Resist the temptation to jump in and bail out the salesperson. Salespeople learn a great deal from rescuing themselves from problems.

- How can you deliver feedback when you play the leading role? When you dominate a sales call, it is your skills, not the salesperson's, that are on display.

- Watch for nonverbal signs. Along with the customer's nonverbal communication, the salesperson's nonverbal communication often speaks louder than words.

- Listen carefully to what is said and what is not said. Can you read between-the-lines nuances that would provide feedback for the salesperson?

Post-call

- Debrief immediately after the call. Do not wait for the end of the day to unload your shopping list of observations. Half of your observations will not make sense at that point.

- Refer to the pre-call questions and ask the salesperson if he achieved them. Pay attention to the action objective.

- Perform an autopsy. What killed the sale? More importantly, why did the salesperson get the business (if the sale was made)?

- Give feedback on the mechanics of the sales call: warm opening, probing for needs, presentation of benefits, and closing.

- Comment on the dynamics of selling: rapport and relationship building, differentiating the solution, trust; momentum, and flow of the call.

How can you provide more effective feedback on sales calls?

_____

_____

_____

Sales Representative Skills Analysis

Use these ideas to deliver standardized feedback to your salespeople after the sales call. This will formalize your coaching and direct your salespeople to become more effective and efficient.

Call preparation

- Was the sales representative prepared for the call?
- Did he or she have all the materials for the presentation?
- Did he or she answer the call-preparation questions?
- Was the itinerary well planned?

During call

- How did the salesperson open the sales call?
- Did the salesperson create rapport with the buyer?
- Did the salesperson engage in an appropriate amount of small talk?
- Did the salesperson state his or her call objective?
- Regarding the questions that the salesperson asked:
  - Were they open versus closed?
  - Did the buyer elaborate?
  - Was there an organized flow?
  - Did the questions make sense in the order in which they were asked?
  - Were the questions penetrating and insightful?
- Did sales representative listen verbally?
- Did sales representative listen nonverbally?

- Were features and benefits relevant and tailored?
- How involved was the prospect at this point?
- Did the sales representative respond to nonverbal clues and buying signals?
- How often did sales representative ask for the business?
- Was the sales representative prepared for objections and how effectively did she handle these objections?
- Did the sales representative achieve his call objective?

Call Effectiveness

This is a measure of quantity and quality of the salesperson's calling efforts. Ask these questions and share your feedback with the salesperson:

- Is this salesperson making enough calls and enough of the right kind of sales calls?
- Is this salesperson making productive sales calls? This is another way of asking, "Is this salesperson making calls or sales?"
- Is this salesperson calling on the right type of customer?
- What results does this salesperson get?

Ten Ways To Deliver Corrective Feedback

One of the great challenges of coaching is delivering the type of feedback that no one enjoys—corrective feedback. Some people call it negative feedback or criticism. Many coaches dislike this part of their job because of the potential for bad outcomes from this type of feedback. This is where courage and assertiveness play a major role in coaching. Ineffective coaches shy away from this responsibility and allow potentially good salespeople to struggle because the coach did not have the intestinal fortitude to direct his or her salespeople down the path of success. These ideas will help you deliver growth-oriented corrective feedback.

- Identify the behavior that you want to criticize. Be clear from the start what you are coaching.
- Criticize the behavior, not the person. Target the actions, not the individual. Salespeople will be less defensive if they feel you are focusing on what they did and not who they are.
- Be clear on why something is a problem. Make sure the salesperson understands why you are raising the issue.
- Be specific. Avoid generalizations like, "You always miss paperwork deadlines" Instead try, "You missed the January 10 deadline for your activity report."
- Make sure the behavior you criticize can be changed. If it cannot be changed, your feedback frustrates the salesperson and obscures the mission. For example, if your salesperson is introverted, it is unrealistic to think this person will become the life of the party. What you can focus on is how this salesperson develops one-on-one relationships with customers.
- Use "we" to reinforce that you want to help jointly fix the problem.
- Do not belabor the point. Keep it short and sweet. Express your complaints and get on with positive recommendations.
- Avoid anger and sarcasm. They are counterproductive. If you must vent your frustration, do it respectfully and explain the frustration. Use this as an opportunity to teach your salesperson how to control impulse anger. You cannot deal with someone else's emotions if your own are spiraling out of control.

- Acknowledge his or her feelings. Salespeople need not apologize for how they feel. That is a fundamental human right. When you make them defend their feelings versus explain their feelings, they can become agitated and your coaching session takes a negative turn.

- When finishing, demonstrate your support and confidence in the other person. Try to end the session with something positive so the salesperson feels this support. Remember, coaching is for the salesperson's benefit.

The biggest tragedy in America is not the great waste of natural resources, though that is tragic. The greatest tragedy is the waste of human resources. The average person goes to his grave with his music still in him. (Oliver Wendell Holmes)

Plateaued Salespeople

One of the most frequent questions sales managers ask is, "How do I deal with a salesperson that is in a comfort zone?" One in four salespeople are in a comfort zone, and 96.5% of companies report that plateaued salespeople are a problem for their companies. So, it is really more of a *when* than *if* issue for most sales coaches. Do you have salespeople who are in comfort zones? Of course you do. Use this checklist with your salespeople to discuss the signs that they may be in a comfort zone.

How do you know if you are in a comfort zone?

- You cannot remember the name of the last book you read on sales.
- Your work needs to be corrected and redone.
- Your follow-through is poor.
- You are working fewer hours.

- You resist management systems and paperwork.
- You live in the past.
- Your paperwork is often late.
- Your absenteeism has increased.
- Everything feels repetitive and too predictable.
- You feel weighed down or trapped by responsibilities.
- You have adopted a more passive attitude.
- You feel low energy, initiative and enthusiasm.
- You have become indecisive and withdrawn.
- Procrastination is more common now.
- You are not generating new ideas.
- Self-sabotaging behavior is more common.
- You are not establishing and pursuing goals.
- You do only what is required.
- Other people have noticed an increase in your cynical comments.
- Everything is resented because it impinges on your time.
- You feel like you are coasting.
- You have downgraded objectives.

(Note to salespeople: If you score seven or more, you are definitely in a comfort zone.)

In many cases, plateaued salespeople are under-challenged. They can execute their jobs while on autopilot. What they have done in the past to get to where they are now will not propel them to the next level. They need to reach beyond their immediate grasp to grow. In some cases, these salespeople have ceased doing what got them to where they are now. For example, cold calling. Some may be in a comfort zone because they lack the energy to get to the next level. Some may be genuinely happy and content where they are.

While some salespeople may be afraid of trying to reach new levels because they fear failure, others may fail to reach new heights because they fear success. Success brings with it the expectation of ongoing effort. If you are successful this year, your company will expect you to be successful next year and the year after that. Some salespeople would rather have a good excuse for not achieving than a good opportunity to succeed. For whatever reason your salespeople are stuck in a comfort zone, you can help them reach for the next level by employing these ideas.

- Encourage them to dream. There is nothing that lifts someone out of a funk quicker than a great big old dream, a dream big enough to make their bones itch!

- Help them maximize and internalize control for their success. I use a two-minute drill in my seminars where I have salespeople list all of the reasons or things that account for their success. At the end of the two minutes, they read aloud their ideas. Invariably, 80% of the things that account for their success are things over which they have some control. The light bulb goes on, and they realize that they control their destiny.

- Encourage your salespeople to read, study, and become serious students of our profession. Have them prepare a report for something they have read, and have them present it at a sales meeting.

- Consider a mentor program where you can use senior salespeople to mentor junior salespeople, provided the senior salespeople are willing to let go of some of their bad habits. The rookies learn from the veterans' experiences, and the senior salespeople draw from the rookie's enthusiasm.

- Have your plateaued salespeople brag about their successes. Spotlight and celebrate these successes. Let them feel the energy of what got them to where they are today. This works especially well when the salesperson gets to brag at a sales meeting in front of his or her peers.

Summary

Coaching is *the* fundamental sales management responsibility. It is the reason you read this book. Coaching is teaching, mentoring, guiding and grading. An effective coach puts the spotlight on the reps. Coaching is for the salesperson's benefit, not yours—even though you benefit from it long-term. Coaching is an all-the-time, anyplace activity. You coach on-the-spot and behind-the-scene. As coach, you provide two types of feedback: quantitative and qualitative. Quantitative feedback tells how much the salesperson is accomplishing. Qualitative feedback tells how well the salesperson is performing. Plateaued salespeople present a special challenge for coaches, and you have it within your power to help these salespeople get to the next level.

To get the most value from this chapter, write your action steps for using these ideas.

_____

_____

_____

CHAPTER EIGHT: TEAMWORK

Value-Added Selling is a team sport. The sales force may sell the first experience with your company, but it is the total experience with your company that brings customers back. If you want to create a value added sales culture, your motto should be, "We is greater than me."

This chapter is about teamwork and what you as the coach can and should do to create and support this culture of value added serving. John Donne wrote, "No man is an island, entire of itself; every man is a piece of the continent, a part of the main…" No one salesperson is greater than the team.

Teamwork is the difference between music and noise. Imagine what would happen if a group of musicians decided that each of them would play simultaneously any song they desired. It would not resemble anything like music. It would be the worst cacophony one can imagine. Music comes from harmony—all elements of the team on the same note of the same sheet of the same song at the same time. This is teamwork.

Teams fail when there is too much me and not enough we. Teams succeed when there is more we than me.

For you to create a value added sales culture, you need all elements of your team playing in concert with each other. Organizational excellence is the natural outcome of individual and team excellence. How your salespeople do their jobs, work with their peers, and interface with customers determine the level at which your company competes.

Synergy

Synergy is the dynamic force of all the pieces working together. This energy force is greater than the sum total of the individual pieces working independently. Collective strength is greater than all the individual strengths put together. Jack Welch, legendary CEO of GE, said, "None of us is even close to being as smart as all of us." Synergy is your collective strength and effort. Consider the power of an entire sales organization focused on the value added sales message and executing in concert.

One of the things I see often in the companies that I work with is the *silo effect*. This is where one department views other departments as the enemy. They view themselves as being in constant competition with other departments for recognition and resources. They do not cooperate. In extreme cases, they sabotage each other. With all of the competition your sales force has on the streets, do you really need competition inside your walls? No. It is wasted energy. Synergy produces music. The silo effect produces noise.

In what ways has the silo effect hurt your sales culture?

_____

_____

_____

Why Teams Fail

Several things cause teams to fail. If your goal is to build a value added sales culture, you need a strong team of individuals who function independently and interdependently. Here are a few things that destroy your efforts at teamwork.

Selfishness

Not sharing credit—individuals who want the spotlight for themselves, not for the team. These people are more interested in personal than team success.

Hoarding information—this is keeping vital information secret as a power play. Others could benefit from this information, but the hoarder is more concerned about personal gain.

Creating a job for oneself—the focus is more on "me" versus "we." This is the opposite of teamwork and demands immediate corrective action by you.

Sabotaging

Secrecy—this is similar to hoarding but broader in its application. For example, holding a meeting where some team members are invited and others are intentionally left out. This becomes a wedge issue for the team.

Passive aggressiveness—this is letting others fail when you could step in to intervene and help out. It is watching team members walk into a minefield and saying nothing to prevent the catastrophe.

Sharp-shooting—taking random pot shots at a team member is intended to lower their status while elevating the sharp-shooter's status. How is this good for teamwork?

Discounting another's values and ideas—this demonstrates a lack of respect for their input. It also smacks of arrogance—that the only good ideas are your ideas.

Attributing motives—it is difficult to second-guess what is in another person's heart. Knowing someone else's motivation is next to impossible, and speculation adds little value to the team.

Mission creep

When your team loses its way, mission creep is generally the culprit. You and the team have failed to lock in on the mission and lock out the distractions. For example, if your mission is to become a value added sales culture and you are doing well but have a slow month, resist the temptation to go for volume with plans to return to the value added approach next month. It confuses your reps; they are drawn off their mission to help build a value added sales culture.

Infrastructure

Resources—does your team have what it needs to do the job? Are you asking them to play a concert, but you are not giving them the instruments they need to make the music?

Systems—do your policies, procedures, systems, and technologies support your team mission? Those things you do that add cost without value diminish your efforts. It is like driving with one foot on the brake and one foot on the gas.

Time—will you give your team the time it needs to accomplish the mission or are you sabotaging their efforts from the start? Encourage your team members to remain focused on the value added sales mission and to fill their days with priorities that support this mission.

Why Teams Succeed

Mission

Clarity—do your salespeople understand what is expected of them to achieve your mission? Is it clear? How often do you communicate this mission to them?

Commitment—are they fully committed to the mission? Do they embrace this mission as their own?

Plan—do you have a plan for accomplishing your mission and have you explained it to your sales force?

Focus—what will you do to keep your salespeople focused on the mission? You want them to lock in on the mission and lock out the distractions.

Balanced participation

Everyone pulls their load—for your team to perform at its peak, everyone must do their part. Resentment follows when a few team members do more than their share. Have you ever had a day when you felt like you were doing all the work yourself and no one cared or helped out. You wanted to turn to the group and say, "Get out of the wagon and help me pull this thing!" That feeling so overwhelmed me one year that I wrote a leadership book by the same title.

Leadership is the process of influencing others to accomplish the mission by providing purpose, direction, and motivation…good leaders recognize how peers, seniors, subordinates work together to produce successes. (Military Leadership Manual, Department of the Army)

Everyone shares in the decision process—even though you may not use their ideas in the final decision, you want their input. No one has a monopoly on great ideas; your team may surprise you with their creativity. The more you listen to them, the greater their commitment to the process.

Clearly defined team roles utilize individual strengths—everyone has a role to play in the success of the team. Make sure you use the talents of each team member. Give them the opportunity to bring value as their strengths allow.

Everyone knows what is expected—do your salespeople know what you expect from them? Remember what we said in the chapter on motivation: People rise or fall to the level of expectations set for them.

There must be a team leader—you are the team leader for your sales force. Ultimately, you are responsible for their success and failure.

Team attitude

Willingness to subordinate egos—your team members must be willing to set aside their personal agendas for the greater good of accomplishing your mission.

Mutual trust and respect—do your team members trust and respect each other? Respect and trust go hand-in-glove. To gain the respect and trust of others, your team members must demonstrate trust and respect to their peers.

Frank, open communications—do your team members feel they can speak openly about team issues and the mission?

Problem-solving attitude—this is the attitude-of-gratitude, where your team feels that it is a privilege to serve as a team member.

Ground rules

Everyone has value—as team leader, your role is to promote and reinforce the belief that all team members are valuable. This encourages mutual respect and trust.

Attack problems, not people—team members can be as aggressive as they want in pursuing solutions to problems. Coach them to reserve their aggressiveness for the problems, not each other.

Listen fully to others' ideas without judging—because of their mutual respect, team members must listen to each others' ideas without passing judgment. Prejudging ideas destroys creativity and involvement.

Value Added Sales Process™ Review

The Value Added Sales Process™ is a cooperative effort and a blend of offensive and defensive selling strategies. Salespeople bring in business, but it is the total experience with a company that affects customer satisfaction, retention and loyalty. This sales-and-operations teamwork is a powerful dynamic force in your company. As the sales coach, you must actively work to foster this teamwork among your salespeople and their internal customers and peers. Your guidance will direct the salespeople toward the business you want to pursue and acquire. Your leadership will inspire the team to work as hard to retain the business as they did to acquire it.

Summary

Value-Added Selling requires teamwork. The sales force may bring in the first piece of business with a customer, but it is the total experience with a company that encourages customers to return and bring friends with them. Teams fail when there is too much me and not enough we. Teams succeed when there is more we than me. Synergy is the collective strength of your team members working together toward a common goal. The silo effect occurs when one department views all other departments as the enemy. As team leader, you are ultimately responsible for the success and failure of your team.

To get the most value from this chapter, write your action steps for using these ideas.

_____

_____

_____

CHAPTER NINE:
WHERE TO FROM HERE?

You have traveled on quite a journey in this book. You have learned how to create the value added sales culture. Specifically, you have learned how to build a value added sales management infrastructure by:

- Evaluating the types of sales positions you need for your team and recruiting candidates that fit your needs, achieve your company's mission and accomplish your departmental objectives.

- Setting objectives that support your mission to become a value added sales culture.

- Training your salespeople to perform the duties of Value-Added Selling.

- Compensating your salespeople equitably and consistently with your goal of becoming a value added sales culture.

- Motivating your salespeople to achieve your goals and accomplish your mission.

- Coaching your salespeople to reach their full potential.

You have learned to think, plan, and execute strategically; how to get the MOST™ from your salespeople; and how to lead your team. In the next section, you will find readings that support your coaching efforts. The follow-up discussion questions that appear after these readings will help you train your sales force on Value-Added Selling. Good luck on your journey to become a sales coach and to create a value added sales culture.

FOLLOW-UP EXERCISES

I designed this section to be used by sales managers to help get the message to their salespeople. This section contains enough material for you to conduct sixteen Value Added Sales training sessions with your salespeople. These sessions walk your salespeople through the Value Added Sales Process™ I introduced you to earlier in the book. Please feel free to copy the readings and the follow-up discussion questions to distribute to your salespeople before the meeting. Then, you can use these readings and questions for your follow-up training session.

SALES PROFESSIONALISM

So, you want to become a professional? As humans, our destiny is to grow, to develop, and to evolve. We aspire to be better. Entire industries are built on the fundamental belief that people want to get better. This is the premise behind billion-dollar industries like healthcare, diet & fitness, and education. Human beings have a burning desire to be better today than yesterday and better tomorrow than today.

As we continue to evolve personally, our work evolves. No job is the same as it was ten years ago; technology took care of that. We live in an information age. Becoming more professional in your job has multiple benefits, both intrinsic and extrinsic. By growing in your job you experience the intrinsic satisfaction of doing the job well. It's fun to excel. It feels good to operate at the top of your game. Extrinsically, you're more competitive, productive, and you add more value to the solution your company offers.

Personal effectiveness precedes professional competency, but since none of us lives in a vacuum, interpersonal effectiveness is the link between individual ability and professional achievement. To become more professional in your career, you must become more personally and interpersonally effective and professionally competent.

Professionalism

At a gut level, we all know what it means to be a professional and we see it in all walks of life: law, medicine, sports, teaching, business, and other fields. A service technician repairs your office copier and people say, "The guy is a real pro." We form our perceptions about professionalism by the way someone carries him or herself—a blend of attitude, knowledge, and performance.

The dictionary defines a professional as someone who is "engaged in a specialized field ... having great skill or experience in a particular field or activity ... one who has assured competence in a particular field or occupation." It further defines a profession as, "an occupation or vocation requiring training and advanced study in a specialized field."

Synonyms that describe professionals include words like: skilled, knowledgeable, experienced, seasoned, trained, adept, gifted, masterful, and proficient. All of these apply to salespeople. A salesperson who operates at the top of his or her game is a professional.

Personal Effectiveness

Effectiveness in time management parlance means working on the right stuff. Personal effectiveness is achieving your goals or producing the anticipated outcome. Sales effectiveness is creating the desired results for your company, your customers, and yourself. Personal effectiveness presumes a desire to grow, learn, change, and perform at the top of one's profession. It's a blend of motivation and know-how. You must possess good personal habits and the knowledge of the task you are charged with performing. Sales effectiveness requires technical knowledge of your product and/or service and the necessary selling techniques to help you engineer the sale.

Interpersonal Effectiveness

John Donne wrote, "No man is an island…" None of us achieves success without the help of other people. That help may come in varying degrees, but it is synergy of your team that continues to reinforce the fundamental business reality: We is greater than me. None of us individually is as strong or as smart as we are collectively. You may reach certain heights on your own, but to soar among the best of the best, you must work well with others. This is interpersonal effectiveness. Personal effectiveness, we said, is how well you know yourself, strengths and weaknesses. Interpersonal effectiveness in how well you know and work with others and understanding the impact you have on other people. You may be the most skilled technician in your field, but without the necessary interpersonal skills, you will never achieve your full potential.

Professional Competence

Being competent is being qualified and capable of performing at an acceptable level. Professional competence is your fitness for operating at a high level of one's vocation. Sales competencies are the right blend of attitudes, attributes, skills, knowledge, and behaviors that contribute to superior performance in your job. These competencies are divided into two categories: how you approach your job and how you interact with people.

Job competencies include proficiency in these areas: product, company and industry knowledge, planning and organizing, recognizing viable sales opportunities, identifying buyer's needs, designing proposals, persuading others to accept your solution, negotiating, closing, resolving objections, following up, time management, and defensive selling.

Inventories

The following inventories will help you assess your personal and interpersonal effectiveness and professional competency. Use this self-assessment to design your follow-up action plan for your personal growth and development. To interpret your scores on these inventories and to use them for personal growth and development, focus on the scores that appear on the lower end of the scale. These are areas that require the most attention.

Personal Effectiveness Inventory

		Low				High
1.	Conceptual thinking and grasp	1	2	3	4	5
2.	Analytical thinking and detail orientation	1	2	3	4	5
3.	Problem solving ability	1	2	3	4	5
4.	Openness to new ideas	1	2	3	4	5
5.	Change-orientation	1	2	3	4	5
6.	Risk-orientation	1	2	3	4	5
7.	Creativity	1	2	3	4	5
8.	Introspection	1	2	3	4	5
9.	Resilience/persistence	1	2	3	4	5
10.	Drive/determination	1	2	3	4	5
11.	Decisiveness	1	2	3	4	5
12.	Goal-orientation	1	2	3	4	5
13.	Initiative/proactive	1	2	3	4	5
14.	Work ethic	1	2	3	4	5
15.	Personal growth/development	1	2	3	4	5
16.	Ability to set priorities	1	2	3	4	5
17.	Focus	1	2	3	4	5
18.	Self-awareness	1	2	3	4	5
19.	Thoroughness and follow-through	1	2	3	4	5
20.	Competitiveness	1	2	3	4	5
21.	Desire for excellence	1	2	3	4	5
22.	Optimistic/can-do attitude	1	2	3	4	5

Interpersonal Effectiveness Inventory

	Low				*High*
1. Empathy	1	2	3	4	5
2. Team attitude	1	2	3	4	5
3. Willingness to serve	1	2	3	4	5
4. Customer-orientation	1	2	3	4	5
5. Listening/nonverbal listening	1	2	3	4	5
6. Ability to communicate ideas—verbal	1	2	3	4	5
7. Written communication	1	2	3	4	5
8. Leadership	1	2	3	4	5
9. Assertiveness	1	2	3	4	5
10. Cooperation	1	2	3	4	5
11. Conflict resolution	1	2	3	4	5
12. Supportive	1	2	3	4	5
13. People reading	1	2	3	4	5
14. Adaptability	1	2	3	4	5
15. Influence	1	2	3	4	5
16. See others' point of view	1	2	3	4	5
17. Internal selling within your company	1	2	3	4	5
18. Relationship building	1	2	3	4	5

Professional Competence

	Low				High
1. Product knowledge	1	2	3	4	5
2. Company knowledge	1	2	3	4	5
3. Industry knowledge	1	2	3	4	5
4. Customer knowledge	1	2	3	4	5
5. Technology knowledge	1	2	3	4	5
6. Plan strategy/organize	1	2	3	4	5
7. Time management	1	2	3	4	5
8. Territory management	1	2	3	4	5
9. Prospect—meet new people	1	2	3	4	5
10. Recognize viable sales opportunities	1	2	3	4	5
11. Identify customer needs	1	2	3	4	5
12. Brainstorm/design solution	1	2	3	4	5
13. Proposal development	1	2	3	4	5
14. Persuading buyers	1	2	3	4	5
15. Resolving objections	1	2	3	4	5
16. Negotiating win/win outcome	1	2	3	4	5
17. Closing	1	2	3	4	5
18. Follow up	1	2	3	4	5
19. Assuring satisfaction	1	2	3	4	5
20. Leveraging/cross-selling	1	2	3	4	5
21. Value reinforcement	1	2	3	4	5
22. Re-creating value post-sale	1	2	3	4	5

Discussion Questions

- Describe your job in detail.
- How is your performance evaluated?
  Quantitative—e.g. sales quota or number of calls
  Qualitative—e.g. the quality of your sales calls or self-development
- What are your sales goals?
- On a personal effectiveness level, what do you need to do and what must you learn to become more effective?
- On an interpersonal effectiveness level, what do you need to do and what must you learn to become more effective?
- On a professional competence level, what do you need to do and what must you learn to become more professional?

HOW TO DETERMINE YOUR COMPANY'S VALUE ADDED

Look at all three dimensions of value: your product, your company, and yourself. First, product value added is what your product does—its impact on the customer. Identify your product value added by considering how your product enhances or improves the following for the customer: profitability, operational efficiency, productivity, performance, quality, safety, ease of use, waste, uptime, durability, consistency, reliability, operating costs, warranty, serviceability, convenience, compliance to specifications, and timeliness.

How does your product add value to your customer's product? Does this product synergy increase competitiveness, attractiveness, and end-user acceptance? How do customers perceive your product—as an investment or an expense? The product dimension of your value added solution is, at best, one-third the value that the customer receives.

The second dimension of value is company value added. Make a list of the value added extras your company provides. This list contains both quantitative and qualitative value added. It includes literature, reputation, industry leadership, facilities, technical support, location, systems, depth and breadth of inventory levels, shipping policies, ordering options, ease of doing business, distribution channels, field support, Internet support, electronic commerce, free delivery, hours of operation, customer loyalty programs, disposal, trade-in policy, and so on. When designing this list, go for quantity initially and then fine-tune it.

Get input from many people. Brainstorm with your peers and your boss. Those employees delivering the value added are closer to the value added than you, and it's on their minds. Others in your company may be able to articulate this value added for you.

Finally, the third dimension of value is your performance—how you, as the salesperson, represent a source of value for the customer. The easiest way for you to determine your value added is to make a list of all the things you do for the customer from the moment a need exists up to and including complete need satisfaction. This could include your conducting an in-depth needs analysis, offering transitional product training, and guaranteed follow-up.

In the planning phase, you may add value by conducting an in-depth needs analysis, providing a live demonstration of your product, studying the buyer's needs and brainstorming a solution, locating hard-to-find items for the buyer, and submitting a professional proposal.

In the transition phase, you may add value by assuring smooth, painless, and seamless transitions to your product. Your value added activities include confirming order status, expediting, tracking backorders, providing training for employees, following the supply chain, and helping with credits and returns.

In the usage (transformation) phase, you add value by following up to assure maximum performance and economy from your product. This post-sale support, coupled with helping customers' businesses grow, differentiate you from all other salespeople with whom they meet. Present this chronology of value added as a flow chart to describe how you will support them from cradle to grave.

Armed with this value added information from each dimension of value you're ready to create your VIP List. Make a list of twenty four value added extras that your total package offers the customer. Be sure to include product value, company value, and salesperson value.

VIP List

Please list twenty Value Added extras you offer

1. _____
2. _____
3. _____
4. _____
5. _____
6. _____
7. _____
8. _____
9. _____
10. _____
11. _____
12. _____
13. _____
14. _____
15. _____
16. _____
17. _____
18. _____
19. _____
20. _____

HOW DO YOU PERSONALLY BRING VALUE TO THE CUSTOMER?

Planning Phase	*Transition Phase*	*Usage Phase*

THE POWER OF DISCERNMENT

Its name implies wisdom, but if that's true, it's ageless wisdom for it can be developed early in life. The power of discernment means knowing what's important and what's not important—intuitively knowing what to do and what not to do. In many cases it's listening to your inner voice and your hunches. It's seeing a clear distinction between alternatives. It's a process of separating alternatives and weighing them against the backdrop of personal values and desires.

Peter Drucker said "the mark of a good manager is knowing which projects to work on." But the mark of a great manager is knowing which projects not to work on. This is the power of discernment at work. Michael Dell, founder of Dell Computer Corporation, said it best one day in the Wall Street Journal, "In business, it's easy to say what you're going to do. The tough part of business is saying what you're not going to do."

Those who develop this power of discernment engage in gainful, meaningful, goal-directed behavior. They operate with a strong sense of priority and purpose. They are able to focus on what really matters in life and get there faster with less wasted effort.

Managers must develop this power of discernment if they ever plan to become strong leaders. Leaders have acquired this power of discernment and they share their wisdom with the troops. Because of their strong sense of mission, they are able to communicate to the troops what's important and what's not.

The power of discernment seems to emanate from the inside out. It begins at our very core—knowing who we are and who we are not. From that, we are able to discern what fits in with who we are and what is at odds with us as well. You can see how useful and necessary this is in business.

Before a company can establish a set of goals or strategy to achieve those goals, it must begin with a strong sense of "who the company is and who the company is not." This inner identity is more fundamental than even the mission statement. The mission statement should support the corporate identity. This strong sense of "who your company is" paves the way for making these types of discernment calls:

- Who we are and who we are not.
- Who our customers are and who they are not.
- Who our competition is and who it is not.
- The kind of business we want to pursue and the kind we want to avoid.
- The things we will do to gain business and the things we will not do.
- The people we will hire and the people we will not hire.
- Where we must invest our resources and where we must ignore investing our resources.
- When to get in a business and when to get out.

Fundamentally, you're making the determination, "What's important to us and what is not?"

Imagine the impact on your organization if every one of your employees, including your salespeople, shared this clarity of identity. Your focus would rival even the most powerful laser beam. You would invest resources for maximum return. You would aggressively pursue only business that would give you the margins you desire. You would design projects and implement policies that added value to your life.

The savings in wasted effort and inefficiencies would astound you. Your organization would be the envy of every competitor. All of this is within your reach by answering a simple question, "Who are we?"

Discussion Questions

- What does the power of discernment mean to you?
- What type of business do you want to pursue?
- What type of business do you want to avoid?
- Who are your six best customers?
- What are your viability criteria for good business?
- Considering all of the above, please name six accounts that fit this profile and why.
- What does each segment want in a solution?
- On what kind of business foundation do you want to build your future?

HI-LEVEL ACCOUNT PENETRATION

Hi-level Value-Added Selling is selling at the highest levels in an account. It is a philosophy of partnerships and value creation for the customer. Calling on the High-Level Decision Maker (HLDM) means talking to someone who has the ability to say "Yes" and "No" to your idea. Generally, it is an upper management type. They create budgets for ideas they like and pull the plugs on projects they feel are a waste of their resources.

Calling on the HLDM shortens your sales cycle, gets you better treatment throughout the account, and creates additional pull for your idea. Besides, there is less competition at the top because most salespeople are too intimidated to call on the HLDM. And when was the last time you heard an HLDM say, "I don't think there's enough budget money for this idea I really like."

Since calling higher in accounts makes sense, we questioned a group of salespeople to determine why they failed to call higher in their accounts. Here is what they told us, "I'm afraid that I will offend my lower-level contact." This was the most common response followed by, "They won't see me." and "I'm intimidated by the HLDM." Lack of confidence, knowledge, or skills seems to hold back most salespeople from calling on the HLDM.

The first step in selling the HLDM is to understand their personalities. They are direct—do not take it personally. They like to control meetings, processes, and decisions. Power is important to them. They take measured risks and make calculated decisions. They are visionaries who live their passion, and their success is often tied to their ability to induce others to follow. Consequently, they are strong leaders. Time is one of their most important resources and they will measure your value by your sense of priority and efficiency.

The things that irritate them are excessive chit-chat, fire hose feature-benefit presentations, not understanding their business, canned presentations, and trying to close too early. They do not want to conduct business with salespeople who have a "transaction" mentality. They want to establish business partnerships with people who are more interested in making a difference than just making a deal.

HLDMs are accessible! You can penetrate accounts at the highest levels. These ideas will help you gain access. One, use an internal referral inside the account. Have that person make a call, send a note to the HLDM, or set up the meeting for you. You might be able to do this with an external referral also.

Two, use a well-written sales letter to break the ice. I call this an Antifreeze Letter (see our letters guide). It takes the chill off the cold call and positions you above the crowd.

Three, arrange for a partnership meeting between your management and the HLDM with whom you want to meet. Two-thirds of HLDMs report that they like this approach. Discuss this with your management.

Four, send a creative mailer and use overnight mail to spotlight it. This mailer should demonstrate your creativity and value. Your willingness to customize it also sets you apart from the competition.

When Meeting With the HLDM

Respect their time. These are busy, productive people who use time as a weapon and view it as a limited resource. Be on time and efficient.

Minimize the small talk. Beyond the cordial formalities of introductions, they do not want to discuss the weather or race to the super bowl.

Deliver high-end leave behinds. A binder that has been customized for this meeting is a great idea because it demonstrates your preparation and thoroughness.

Research their organizations thoroughly. Visit their web sites and read their annual reports. Pay attention to page two of the annual report. It speaks to their vision. Demonstrate your knowledge of their organization early in the meeting.

Ask questions that reflect higher level needs. Ask about their mission, vision, outside pressures, market trends, employee issues, resource allocation, etc.

Present high-level solutions. Support their mission and contribute to their critical success factors.

HLDMs are decisive, action-oriented individuals. They got to where they are by focusing on and creating results. If they believe in you and your solution, they will be a strong influence in making it happen in their organization.

Discussion Questions

- Are you talking to all the right people?
- What have you experienced by penetrating accounts late in the decision process?
- What's the advantage of getting in early?
- Who do you call on when you penetrate the account?

- Who can create pull; i.e. be your internal champion, in the account?
- Who are the typical high-level decision makers (HLDMs) with whom you do business?
- How effective have you been in penetrating HLDMs?
- Who are the HLDMs in your top six accounts?
- Do you have relationships with them?
- How do you need to establish relationships with them?
- How does your company's solution appeal to HLDMs?
- How do you appeal to all levels of decision makers?
- Who are your . . .
  - Level I contacts?
  - Level II contacts?
  - Level III contacts?
- Do you have collateral material for each of the above?
- What would be the best way to arrange for connections at all levels in the client's organization?

CUSTOMER-IZING: LEARNING TO THINK AS CUSTOMERS THINK

A fundamental principle of Value-Added Selling is that buyers, not sellers, define value. Too many companies encourage their salespeople to create a need for what they sell versus understanding the buyer's need and then creating a solution. Eighty percent of sales training dollars are spent on teaching product knowledge. Salespeople interpret this as how they should spend time with buyers—talking versus listening. This translates into fire hose, feature-benefit presentations in which the salesperson dominates the conversation—a monologue, not a dialog.

Customer-izing is learning how to think as buyers think— defining value in customer's terms. It's developing an in-depth understanding of the buyer's needs and the driving forces behind these needs. It's seeing life from the buyer's unique point of view.

Organizational Needs

Buyers have a complex set of needs that include both organizational and individual influences. I like to use the analogy of the iceberg to illustrate this point. The tip of the iceberg represents the obvious—the visible needs. The buyer uses these objective buying criteria to evaluate competitive alternatives. The buyer attempts to satisfy this set of needs when making a buying decision.

Organizational needs include compliance to specifications, quality, delivery, terms, price, product performance, ordering convenience, and other fundamental buying criteria. To fully understand these needs, ask yourself these questions:

- What are your buyer's total organizational needs for a solution?
- What is your buyer's decision process?
- How is the power base distributed throughout your buyer's organization?
- What opportunity areas exist?
- What are your buyer's critical issues for this particular purchase?

Collectively, these various needs compose your customer's organizational profile. This is the tip of the iceberg. The less-visible issues are the individual's needs.

Personal Issues

One of the great opportunity areas in business-to-business selling is the human side of the buying decision. There is a tendency for business-to-business salespeople to underestimate the role that emotion plays in the sale. Emotion drives buying decisions. This is true even for the most technical sale. People still buy from people. Human beings are emotional creatures. We make emotional decisions and often use reason to justify them.

Individual involvement in buying decisions is the personal set of needs, wants, desires, and fears that exist beneath the surface in my iceberg analogy. This set of issues is not always visible. In fact, some buyers may attempt to hide these personal needs, wants, and fears. These issues represent a personal win for the buyer. On a personal level for the buyer, they answer the question, "What's in it for me?" An important Value-Added Selling principle is: Buyers prefer to buy what they need from salespeople who understand what they want to achieve and what they want to avoid.

Buyers make emotional decisions based on what they want to achieve and what they want to avoid—gains and pains. Personal gains include the things people want more of: control, image, power, security, stability, ego gratification, greed, and other positives.

Pains or fears include what they want less of: risk, more work to do, too much exposure on something, a call at two o'clock in the morning asking where the supplies are, loss of control, damage to their image, being politically vulnerable, making a mistake, and other negatives.

Selling on both levels—organizational needs and personal wants—gives you a powerful advantage. You create a solution that helps the buyer achieve his or her organizational objectives while satisfying his or her personal goals. Customer-izing is studying this complex set of needs, wants, and fears when you're with the buyer and when you're behind the scenes. Use this information to customize a solution.

Discussion Questions

- Do you know how your customers really think?
- Does your company have a customer value focus?
- What are the organizational needs that your customers typically have?
- What are the personal wants and fears in your accounts?
- For your top three accounts, identify the pressure points that are operational at any given time.
- How can you customer-ize your solution to meet the customer's needs, wants, and fears?

WHAT IS POSITIONING?

Positioning is forging an image in the buyer's mind. It's carefully shaping how you want others to perceive you. It's framing your message in a way that supports your communication objective. Positioning is a marketing strategy that salespeople tactically execute to persuade others that their solution is the value added solution.

Value-Added Selling grows from a simple principle: People buy more than a product. They buy all three dimensions of value—the product, the company, and the people. Collectively, this is your solution. What image do you want to project in each of these three areas?

- Product—quality, durability, state-of-the-art technical superiority, and user-friendliness.
- Company—ease-of-doing-business, commitment to innovation, support, management flexibility and stability.
- People—helpful, concerned, informed, and customer-oriented.

To position your solution effectively, you must have a clear understanding of the image you want to communicate. Then you must use marketing to deliver your message. Marketing is every way you communicate with your buyer.

Every salesperson projects an image to the buyer. Does the buyer perceive you as a deal guy who is interested only in the transaction or as someone who is interested in making a difference? Does the buyer view you as an expert in your field? Are you a valuable resource whom the buyer can rely upon?

Factors That Affect Your Personal Position With the Buyer

Knowledge—Seventy-six percent of value added is knowledge-based. Your knowledge can position you as an expert—an important part of the team. One buyer told me that he depends on salespeople for the majority of industry knowledge he gathers. Do your buyers perceive you as a viable source of information?

Appearance—Do you look like a success? Value added salespeople dress to the top of their market. Do you dress for success? Perceived value includes personal packaging in addition to product packaging.

Use of time—Buyers value their time. They also watch how others use time. Successful people use time effectively. Your efficient use of time communicates the image that you respect this valuable resource. Others will respect your time if you respect it.

Personal organization—Do you have it together? Are you organized or agonized? When you make the time to organize your presentation, it shows. When you fail to make the time to organize, it also shows. If you can't keep yourself together, why should buyers think you could pull it together for them?

Communications—How effectively do you communicate your thoughts? Do they make sense to the buyer? Are you easy to follow, or do you ramble incessantly about subjects that bore your buyer?

Presentations—Are they impressive? Are they convincing? Do you present a compelling reason for the buyer to choose your alternative? How much time do you invest in planning for the sales presentation?

Passion—Aristotle recognized that passion sells and enthusiasm is contagious. If you're not excited about what you offer, how can you expect the buyer to get excited?

Sincerity—Buyers want to trust sellers. Sincerity builds this trust. The fundamental question that your buyer asks is, "Can I trust you?"

Success—Do you have a record of success? Nothing sells like success. Buyers like to do business with others who know how to create success. Brag positively. Selective name-dropping works well.

Discussion Questions

- What image have you created in the customer's mind?
- What does positioning mean to you?
- What image do you currently own in the customer's mind in these three areas?
  - Your product
  - Your company
  - Yourself
- What image do you want to project in each of these three areas?
  - Product
  - Company
  - Salesperson
- What are some things you can do behind the scenes to support this image?
- What can you do, face-to-face with the customer, to reinforce your position?
  - Product
  - Company
  - Salesperson
- How does the customer perceive you as a salesperson?

DIFFERENTIATION

Customers fret; suppliers sweat. Buyers make decisions daily about supply alternatives; it's as if each of these buyers has a collage of suppliers hanging on their office wall. The buyer views the collage and tries to select an alternative that stands out. It's harder than it sounds and for good reason. These "four C's" explain why buyers fail to perceive the differences among their suppliers.

Commoditization

The quality revolution ushered in an era of suppliers cleaning up their acts. Buyers tell us in surveys that they prefer higher quality; who sells inferior quality today? Quality has become first-cut criteria. If you don't sell good stuff, buyers don't want to talk to you.

At the same time, look-alike products compound the problem. Suppliers, in an effort to compete, always seek ways to gain competitive advantage and may turn to innovation. Other, less creative, suppliers copy the innovation, and buyers then view the product as a commodity. It increases the buyers' negotiating leverage if they can relegate your product to commodity status.

Convergence

Copying is not limited to products. If one company offers a unique service, it doesn't take long for competitors to copy that service—hence, the convergence of services. Consider the buyers' dilemma: two products appear to have the same core qualities, wrapped in a blanket of identical services. What would you do? I once heard the definition of a commodity as "a product differentiated only by its price."

Consolidation

Buyers want to consolidate purchasing, and sellers are buying and selling each other—i.e. merging—faster than minks reproduce. Sounds simple, except for the fact that consolidation blunts supplier differences. To consolidate means to bring together. How can you have differences when everyone regresses around the mean? The net outcome is a whole lot of superstore-type companies that look alike.

Conformity

Most people spend their whole lives trying to fit in and lose sight of the fact that it's okay to be different. It starts early in life by hanging out with the right crowd, wearing the right clothes, and going to the right schools. Later in life, it means driving the right car, joining the right club, and again, knowing the right people.

Because most of us spend so much time fitting in, we forget that we're supposed to be different. If we weren't meant to be different, why are we made differently? It takes courage to be different—to stand out from the crowd.

In sales, fitting in is the curse of mediocrity. Being different is the essence of competition. How can you compete effectively if you, your company, and your product look like everything else in the market? Over half the salespeople I train cannot tell me why the customer should pay more to buy their product. They fail to answer one of the most fundamental sales questions of all:

What are the definable and defendable differences between you and the competition?

To sell effectively against the competition, use these ideas:

Tip #1: Keep it positive . . . don't go negative. Resist the impulse to bad-mouth the competition. Avoid negative selling at all costs. In an era when politicians trash each other and manufacturers advertise directly against another brand in product comparison studies, avoid the temptation to bad-mouth your competition. When you go negative it says something about you and your style to the customer.

Tip #2: Prepare a Ten-Things-To-Consider List. List ten areas where your product, company and people are superior. It makes it easy for the customer to see the differences between you and the rest of the pack.

Tip #3: Use a comparison matrix. Across the top of the matrix list three or four suppliers. Down the left-hand side of the matrix list a dozen comparison variables. Within each cell of that matrix list the specific advantages each brings to the table.

Tip #4: Get others to sell for you. A technique I have used for years when a customer asks, "Why should I hire you, Tom, versus someone else?" is to give the customer references of other clients who have worked with both of us. I will say "Why not hear first-hand from one of my other customers what they have to say about both of us?"

Tip #5: Acknowledge the generic. You might say something like this to the customer, "When you look at both of our products you will notice a similarity that both of them meet a fundamental need. What I would really like to focus your attention on is those areas in which we really excel." The implication is if you excel in these areas, the competition does not.

Discussion Questions

- What are the definable and defendable differences between you and the competition? What is differentiation?
- What are the primary differences between your company and your top two competitors?
- What are the primary differences between your product and your top two competitors?
- What are the primary differences between your sales reps and your top two competitors?
- How can you sell these differences to the customer?
- In what ways can you create barriers that defy direct comparison?
- When the customer says, "Aren't you and Company B in the same business?" devise your reaction based on the following: "Well, we're in the same industry, but we're not in the same business, and here's why…"
- Why should the customer pay more to do business with your company?

Differentiation Matrix: What are the definable and
defendable differences between you and the competition?

Product Attributes	Our Company	Competitor A	Competitor B
Availability			
Packaging			
Warranty			
Acquisition price			
Quality			
Usage cost			
Durability			
Performance			
Brand name			
Efficiency			
Safety			
User friendly			
Company Attributes			
Ease of doing business			
Reputation			
Technical support			
Terms			
Return policy			
Inventory levels			
Service policy			
Ordering options			
Management flexibility			
Industry leader			
Post-sale support			
Pre-sale assistance			
Salesperson Attributes			
Knowledgeable			
Follow-through			
Understands needs			
Empathy			
Accessible			
Integrity			
Straight forward			
Innovative			
Good listener			
Eager			
Organized			
Gets things done			

Ten-Things-to-Consider List

In the following spaces, list ten key selling points about the
uniqueness of your solution. Then present this to your customer.

_____

_____

_____

_____

_____

_____

_____

_____

_____

PRESENTING A COMPELLING REASON TO BUY: THE RULE OF THREES

To present a compelling reason for why the buyer should choose your alternative, practice the rule of three's: sell all three dimensions of value; have three quick and relevant benefits to present; and mind the three P's.

The Three Dimensions of Value

Buyers purchase more than a product or service. Along with the product or service, they get the company that supplies that product and the salesperson who sells the product. These are the three dimensions of value: product, company, and people. Be prepared to discuss all three dimensions of value with your customer.

The product offers specific features and benefits. The company offers value in many areas: depth of resources, number of locations, management philosophy, and financial stability. As the salesperson, your knowledge and follow-through are important to the customer. The same products, from the same company, from two different salespeople are two different solutions entirely.

Three Quick-and–Relevant Benefits

Have three quick-and-relevant benefits for why the buyer should consider your alternative. Some people call this a three-minute sales pitch; others call it your elevator speech because it should be the length of a quick elevator ride. When building this three-benefit sales message, consider the three dimensions of value and offer a key benefit in each area. For example, your three-benefit sales message may sound like this:

"Our solution offers your company three important benefits. First, we have seven shipping points located strategically around your warehouses. This will cut your shipping costs in half. Second, our product has an energy monitor governor which controls the amount of energy you need to operate it. This saves you operating costs. Third, because of our guaranteed follow-up policy, I monitor your equipment purchase to ensure you get maximum performance and economy from our products."

The Three P's

These three P's guide your longer presentations: personalizing, perceived value, and performance value.

Personalize your message—Does your message reflect the buyer's definition of value? Are you acting from a customer value focus? Buyers want to feel that you understand their definition of value and have designed a solution that reflects their priorities. This is customer-oriented selling at its best.

Maximize your perceived value—Is it sexy? Does it sizzle? Does it have flash? These are questions to ask yourself about how your stuff looks—your style. Perceived value is the context of your message. It influences the buyer's expectations. It gives buyers a warm and fuzzy feeling about your solution. In order to generate this feeling, every steak must sizzle. Maximizing your perceived value is a quick way to make a positive impact on your presentation. Perceived value is how something looks, feels, and sounds to the buyer. Does it pop? Does it have splash? Does it make the buyer's blood race through his or her veins?

Demonstrate performance value—This answers the question, "Where's the beef?" Performance value is the profit impact you have on the customer's business. It's the steak behind the sizzle, and the quantitative behind the qualitative. While perceived value defines your style, performance value demonstrates your substance. This is the content of your message.

Buyers are bombarded with hundreds of marketing messages every day. For your message to be heard above the roar of the crowd, you must stand out in some fashion. The rule of three's capitalizes on relevance and speed to get your sales message across.

Discussion Questions

- How compelling is your message?
- 3-D message for customer needs. Use the Presentation Planning Matrix.
- In what ways can you personalize your message to make it more relevant to the customer (analogies, etc.)?
- How can you increase your perceived value—the look of things—to customers? How can you more effectively demonstrate your performance value?
- If you were to develop a three-benefit (minute) sales pitch, what are the three most important benefits you offer in these areas:
  - Company
  - Product
  - You, the salesperson
- Is your message customized for your customer's needs?

SERVING AND SUPPORTING

As you begin the supporting phase of the Value Added Sales Process™, you are making a shift from offensive to defensive selling. In offensive selling, you're pursuing new business opportunities. In defensive selling, you're protecting existing business. At this phase of the sale, the customer's greatest need is for smooth, seamless, and painless transitions to your solution. The customer wants to work with salespeople who can make this happen. This is the shift point to defensive selling.

Process Support

This is when you put on your logistics support hat. You've transitioned from sales to service. Here is a sampling of how you add value:

- Verifying order status;
- Expediting orders and chasing backorders;
- Providing substitute shipments;
- Greasing the skids;
- Following the supply chain;
- Handling credits and returns;
- Preparing facilities;
- Receiving and warehousing products;
- Redistributing goods.

To provide the level of support that customers require, you must use your internal selling skills. These are the skills you use to make things happen inside your own company. Working with the credit department to help better serve the customer is internal selling. Convincing the shipping department that packaging flexibility is important to this buyer is internal selling. Selling your manager on the concept of a customer-appreciation golf outing is internal selling. In this logistics support mode, you follow the order from receipt to delivery to assure timeliness and accuracy. Likewise, your customers want seamless and painless transitions to your solution. Your job is to make the path smooth.

For example, I know a heavy-duty truck salesman who is a master of defensive selling. He begins his support by confirming the order to ensure that it is correct. He monitors the progress of the order and provides his customer with periodic updates. When the truck is being prepared for delivery, he conducts a pre-delivery inspection to ensure that the specifications match the order. When the truck is ready for delivery, he performs a walk-around demonstration to ensure that the buyer understands the truck's operating features. If the buyer has any questions on the documentation or registration, the salesman clarifies that information also. This salesman takes great pride in taking care of his customers. He treats each sale as if it were his first sale with this customer.

People Support

Now you are wearing your people hat. You're serving people versus the process. You're a supporter, champion, mediator, ally, partner, trainer, and cheerleader. You're an advocate for the customer and liaison for your company. You are the customer's safety net, hand holder, and therapist all rolled up into one. You provide value as you serve by:

- Introducing cross-functional teams to each other;
- Training as needed;

- Offering technical support;
- Handling inquiries and questions;
- Following up on requests;
- Providing back-up as needed;
- Helping to lighten the load.

Some people might call this the softer support you offer. To the customer, this is as real as it gets. The TLC, handholding, and information you provide reassure customers that they made the correct decision in selecting your alternative. This personalized service-after-the-sale is what continues to position you and your company as the value added solution in the industry. You allay fears and confirm the customer's decision to buy. This eliminates buyer's remorse.

Discussion Questions

- How much support do you offer your customers?
- Describe the shift from offensive to defensive selling in your business.
- What steps can you take to support the customer logistically once they have placed the order?
- How can you make the transition to your company smoother for the customer?
- What type of people support do you offer at the time of ordering and receiving?
- How does your company help customers logistically?
- Who, other than you, should be involved in this support?

SELLING IS RELATIONSHIP MANAGEMENT

This is one of those common-sense ideas that most people accept. It even shows up in job interviews when the candidate is asked, "Why do you want to get into sales?" The candidate responds with, "I'm a people person. I like people." That salespeople like people is a cliché—albeit, an important cliché.

How do most people find employment opportunities? They network, which is a euphemism for schmoozing. It's a contemporary version of the old saying, "It's not what you know in this world that counts, it's who you know that counts."

After twenty years of sales training experience, I have seen some of the least technically-inclined salespeople who were some of the most effective salespeople I've seen—in spite of their lack of technical or tactical proficiency. They get the job done because they possess incredible people skills and are masters of relationship selling. I have witnessed some of these salespeople in role-play scenarios and their tactical performance was abysmal at best. They stumbled and stammered their way through sales calls in training, but seemed to get the job done in the field. How do they do it? In many cases, they have established strong bonds with their customers. They take them hunting, fishing, or golfing.

Their families take vacations with customers' families. Their spouses are great friends with the customers' spouses. These salespeople know as much about their customers' children as they know about their own. Their customers have them on speed dial—not just the office phone number, but home numbers and cell phone numbers.

I met a salesperson in Canada who was so tight with his customers and whose family was so tight with his customers' families that when one customer threatened to purchase two million dollars worth of product somewhere else because of a significant price difference the customer's wife threatened to kick him out of the house. She said, "For everything that man has done for you, how can you go anywhere else? If you give that order to the other salesperson, you can just move out of the house right now." Now, that's pressure! Who wouldn't love to have that type of internal champion pushing their cause?

I know another salesperson who gave up valuable playoff football tickets so that a customer could take his young son to a Rams' football game. The customer appreciated the salesperson's sacrifice and rewarded him with loyalty.

Marketers talk about brand loyalty, but I argue that this term is a misnomer. When I drink beer, there is a brand I prefer. When I buy gasoline for my car, there is a brand I prefer. When I eat bagels, there is a brand I prefer. But I am not loyal to those brands; I prefer them. Loyalty is something I reserve for the people with whom I deal. Loyalty, in my view, is an interpersonal dynamic.

Now, let's be clear on what I'm saying and what I'm not saying. First, are there salespeople who, by virtue of their charisma and interpersonal skills, are able to sell in spite of poor tactical knowledge of how to make a sales call? Yes. Should you model yourself after them? No. They cannot tell you how they do it; they don't know how they do it, as far as sales technique goes. They will immediately go to their people skills and stress the importance of the relationship with their buyers.

Are there salespeople who rely more on selling technique and structure to get the job done? Yes. And I believe the majority of salespeople fit this profile; this is why we offer product and sales training. These salespeople still employ interpersonal skills, but they rely equally on technique.

Relationship management is not reserved for the few who won popularity contests in high school and college. Everyone can work on this dimension of their lives, and it's not restricted to professional relationships. Becoming a better relationship manager, vis-à-vis people skills, rounds out your personality. "We" is greater than "me." Selling is a team sport. And as John Donne said, "No man is an island." We depend on each other. We need each other. If two people like each other, trust each other, and want to do business, they will work out the details; in most cases, price is a detail.

Building stronger relationships with your customers is another dimension to selling that can help you get to the next higher level in this profession. It's also a way for the customer to get to see what kind of person you really are. They want to know that they are dealing with a real-life human being who has feelings, just as they do. You will find that as you build these relationships you will make new friends along the way and touch them in ways that you couldn't have from a distance.

Discussion Questions

- How is your relationship with the customer?
- What does Relationship Selling mean to you?
- Describe why you feel you're in the "people" business.
- How can you build stronger personal relationships with your customers?
- How can you help your customer build their business?
- What type of customer loyalty programs can your company establish?
- How can you demonstrate to your customers how much you value their business?

TINKERING:
THE ESSENCE OF INNOVATION

The implicit promise in Value-Added Selling is your pursuit of excellence; in tinkering, you continuously search for ways to re-create value for your customer. Customers want to feel they are dealing with suppliers who want to grow, evolve, and emerge. They want to buy from sellers who are innovative and who put it all together and then push the change curve.

Tinkering is working as hard to keep the business as you did to get the business. Tinkering is treating your customers as if they were prospects, because they are . . . for the competition. When you tinker, you're doing what a good, quality competitor does to earn the business.

Emerson wrote, "If you build a better mousetrap, the world will beat a path to your door to buy it." The Japanese call this "kaizen"—an attitude of continuous improvement. Seeking to build a better mousetrap is living the "what if" question. "What if we could do it this way?" "What if we could make our product do this?" Every great product innovation is the evolution of another great idea.

Customers want to feel that you're keeping them ahead of the curve with your innovation. Value added peak competitors think forward and visualize endless possibilities, stretching their imaginations to their outer reaches.

You can ask the "what if" question throughout your company and with your customers. My first sales job taught me great habits, among them, how to ask for new product suggestions on sales calls. We had to submit three new product suggestions every month. The only way we could do this was to plow the ground by asking the following questions on every sales call: "What would you like to see from suppliers that is not currently available?" "What would you like to have that you cannot get now?" Even though I worked for one of the oldest companies in the industry, we had some of the most innovative ideas among all our competitors.

How easy is your company to do business with? Do customers use words such as "inflexible," "single-minded," "arrogant," "indifferent," and "seller-focused" to describe your policies and procedures? Or, do they use words such as "flexible," "considerate," "patient," "customer-focused" and "easy to do business with"?

In our value added survey, buyers told us they wanted to work with sellers who made it easy for them to do business. What can you do to make it easier for your customers to order? How does your credit department perceive its role? Does it build bridges to draw people in or build walls to keep the bums out? Are there more convenient ways for your customers to pay for your goods and services? Are there special packaging options that make it easier for your customers to redistribute your goods and services internally? Can you bundle different product groups more efficiently to reflect special buyer needs?

At the heart of this strategy is an attitude that says, "We can and should look for ways to make it easier to buy and use our products." "Painless," "seamless," and "customer-centric" are words that describe the results of your efforts when you tinker to make the customer's life easier.

Even more fundamental is the belief that people continue to grow and develop if they are open to change and humble enough to admit that they aren't finished yet. It's a self-sabotaging form of arrogance to believe that you have no room for growth.

Value added peak competitors are proud of what they have accomplished, but they balance their pride with an equally strong measure of humility that says, "We're not finished yet. We still have some distance to travel."

Discussion Questions

- Are you working as hard to keep the business as you did to get it?
- Why does it make sense to seek ways, on an ongoing basis, to re-create value?
- What is the benefit/advantage of tinkering?
- How can you build a better mousetrap?
- What barriers get in the way of your delivering world-class service?
- How can you make it easier for the customer to do business with your company?
- Can you make a list of improvements for customers?
- Is your company open to tinkering?
- Does your company respond to customer suggestions for enhancements?
- Is tinkering cultural in your company?

VALUE REINFORCEMENT

Most companies I work with bring great value to the table but rarely get credit for everything they do. In most cases, their customers are uninformed about the extent of this value added. You can't fault buyers for taking for granted your added value when they don't know the value of your total solution. But you can highlight this value by using value reinforcement.

Documentation

Are you able to attach a dollar value to the services you offer? Can you calculate the profit impact on the customer's business? How much are you really worth to your customers? The answers to these questions provide the backdrop for the financial justification of your solution.

Documenting value added services proactively manages price resistance. I know a salesperson that uses no-charge invoices to inform the customer of the dollar value of his services. For example, his company once sent two technical people into the field to handle a problem. After they finished this assignment, the salesperson calculated the expense his company incurred, including travel and field time. He sent the customer a no-charge invoice for $4,400. On the bottom of the invoice, in bold print, he typed, "No charge—part of our value added service."

Another client uses a project savings report. When the company completes a technical assignment, it sends a recap of the work and its impact on the customer. This report documents the benefits offered by this supplier. It quantifies the impact so that the customer can appreciate the real dollar difference that results.

Warranty reports detail the value of the work performed under warranty. Many times, customers misunderstand warranty work. They think it's free. I had a problem with brakes on an automobile I was driving. The dealer spent two days repairing the problem. The factory reimbursed the dealer for only 1.8 hours. I paid nothing. The service manager showed me the warranty documentation and said, "Just keep us in mind when you need an oil change."

Value Reminding

Value reminding is positive bragging. It's looking for ways to remind customers of everything you do for them. For example, when the customer calls you for technical support and you must pass this request along to someone else, you should follow up with the customer to ensure satisfaction. It demonstrates your concern while reminding the customer of your service.

If you help a customer secure a piece of business, follow up to see how it benefited the customer. This reinforces that you're working for the customer. Imagine the impact when the customer tells you that your lead resulted in a large sale.

Testimonial letters provide a unique way to reinforce your value added. When the customer writes you a testimonial letter, it's to tell you about the great job you've done. More importantly, the customer is actively remembering the great job you've done. If you want to do something that requires chutzpah, in your next proposal to this customer, include a copy of his or her own testimonial letter to you. Who better to remind the customer of your value added than this very same customer?

Value Audit

The value audit is either a formal or informal way to check on your performance with the customer. Formally, it's a customer satisfaction survey. It could be as detailed as the surveys that auto manufacturers use to measure your buying and owning experience. In the customer satisfaction survey, you measure performance and how it produces buyer satisfaction or dissatisfaction.

A value audit could be as informal as your asking questions in follow-up visits. "Mr. Customer, I wanted to meet with you today to check on ourselves, to ensure that you're getting all the value on the back end that we promised you on the front end. How are we performing for you? How can we improve? What would you like us to do for you tomorrow that we didn't do for you yesterday?"

The best defense is a great offense. By checking on yourself, you're doing what a quality competitor should do when pursuing new business. It's better for you to know your strengths and weaknesses before the competition discovers them.

Discussion Questions

- Are you getting credit for all of your value added?
- Do you get credit for all the value added you bring to the table? Cite examples.
- What are the various value added services that you would like to be recognized for?
- What is the best way to advise customers of the dollar value of these value added extras?
- What other ways can you remind the customer of your value added?
- How do customer satisfaction surveys and audits fit in with your plan?
- Are you currently using value reminding?

THE POWER OF LEVERAGE

You spend an incredible amount of time chasing new business. You finally land the account and what happens? You start this cycle all over again. On average, it takes seven calls to close a new prospect on a new idea but only three calls to close an existing customer on the same idea. It costs ten times more to land a new account than it does to serve an existing customer. So why do you continue to chase all this new stuff to the degree that you ignore existing business?

Because you're told to. There is a national obsession with what I call Pipeline-itis. This is the pursuit of new accounts to the extent that you slight your existing customers. It reminds me of the acres of diamonds speech I heard years ago. It's a story where a young adventurer explores new lands for wealth when in reality he had great wealth on his own land. It's first cousin to the grass-is-always-greener story.

Managers direct salespeople to open new accounts, constantly plant seeds, and pursue new opportunities. Why? Because they're deathly afraid of losing the business they have; therefore, you need to have a lot in the wings. The irony is striking, isn't it?

Many compensation packages are designed to reward salespeople for new business. Sales managers tell me, "We pay fifteen percent on new accounts and ten percent on repeat business." So why do you think salespeople tend to ignore existing accounts in favor of chasing new ones?

Defensive selling is a big part of Value-Added Selling. It's nailing shut the back door so that you don't lose as much business out of the back door as you bring in new business through the front door. It's treating your customers as if they were prospects . . . because they are—for the competition. It's working as hard to keep the business as you did to get it.

Leverage is the principle of achieving a high ratio of outcome to input. It's 150% return on a 100% investment. In defensive selling terms, this means increasing your business with existing customers. I believe that the average company with whom I work can increase sales in a given year by twenty percent, even if they did not bring on board one new account, if they only did a better job of selling to existing customers. They leverage their relationships.

They achieve this by increasing their account penetration—vertically and horizontally. Vertical account penetration is increasing the depth and breadth of what you sell to a given customer—expanding your mix. Ask yourself, "What else should and could I be selling to this customer?" Are you getting all of the residual business that normally goes with a product? Are there other things they buy that you are not selling them? The more levels at which you connect, the more solid the relationship.

Horizontal account penetration is when you sell more locations of the same customer. Do they have more than one office? Are there branch locations? Are there other people in the account that you should call on?

You can leverage your relationships by spin-off referrals. Ask every existing customer this question, "Who else should I be talking with?" Leave it wide open and prepare to take notes. One salesperson went through our five-day seminar and called me a couple of weeks later to tell me that he had asked that question twenty times since the seminar and received eleven solid leads—

three of which were probable sales. He had to quit asking the question because he couldn't follow up on all the leads he was getting from his customers. Not a bad position to be in, is it?

Let's go back to the original point. Why are you spending so much time chasing new customers when existing customers represent the acres of diamonds on your own land?

Discussion Questions

- Are you getting all of the business you should be getting from the account?
- Where is the easiest place to sell something; or who is the easiest personal to sell?
- What are growth areas with existing customers?
- Which customers are your best cross-sell targets?
- Which product lines offer cross-sell opportunities?
- What spin-off business opportunities exist for you either as niches or referrals?
- Are you getting full account penetration?
- How much time do you spend expanding opportunities with existing customers?

PLANNING AND PREPARATION
EQUALS TWICE THE PERFORMANCE

Value-Added Selling is a process, not an event. There are four steps in this ongoing process, and they repeat themselves continuously.

Step one is preparation. Preparation is the getting-ready phase. Planning and preparation equals twice the performance. Focus strategically on the types of customers that will give you the kind of return you're looking for. Be selective in how you allocate your sales time.

Step two is planning. Planning is call-specific. Planning means reviewing what you know about your customer and asking yourself these six pre-call questions.

- What do I want to accomplish on this call?
- What is my probing objective?
- What is my presentation objective?
- What collateral pieces do I need?
- What obstacles do I anticipate?
- What action do I want from the customer at the end of this call?

Complete a call planning guide where you write down your opening, the questions you want to ask, the value added features and benefits you want to stress, and how you'll close the sale.

Step three is call execution. This is your face-to-face meeting with the customer. At least 50% of the time is spent understanding the customer's needs. Begin your value added sales call by asking questions. This must be more of a dialogue, not a monologue. When you tell your value added story, draw the customer into the presentation so it doesn't become one-way communication. When you're finished listening to the customer and telling your story, you must ask for the business.

Step four is follow-up. Follow-up is important, yet often overlooked. In follow-up you never leave the parking lot without scheduling the next action step for this customer. You do a post-call analysis to review your performance. "How did I perform? Did I stay on track?" "Was the chemistry right?" With the information you've acquired on this call, feed it back into the preparation phase to complete the loop for planning future sales calls.

Call Planning Guide

Objectives:

Opening:

Probing:

Presenting:

Closing:

Outcome:

Next Step:

TYPES OF PRICE OBJECTIONS

There are at least six types of price objections. Maybe more. Understanding these will prepare you to deal with the price shopper.

Type One: Focus objections—your buyer's focus could be way off. For example, the buyer may be focusing on acquisition price versus ownership and usage costs. He's obsessing with the cost to buy, the today price—not the cost to own, the tomorrow price. This short-term time horizon is typical of price shoppers.

Apples-to-oranges comparisons are a focus problem. The buyer chooses the incorrect comparison standard. The product to which he compares your product may not be in the same food group.

Your strategy in dealing with focus objections is to help the buyer focus more clearly on the relevant issues.

- Stretch the buyer's time horizon to make him aware of long-term issues.
- Educate the buyer on competitive differences. "We might be in the same industry as our competitor but we're not in the same business and here's why..."

Type Two: Information-based objections—the buyer may lack the information he needs to make a buying decision that favors your product. There are situations when the buyer has inadequate information about his needs. He may not know what he needs and why he needs it.

He may have low expectations about price because of his naiveté in the marketplace. You've seen this before. It's called sticker shock.

The buyer may lack enough relevant information about your product and company to feel your package is worth the price. She's just not sold on you. If the buyer lacks information, your strategy is to:

- Help the buyer develop a deeper understanding of his or her needs.
- Give the buyer time to adjust to the sticker price. It may only take a few days to modify these expectations.
- Educate the buyer about the total value of your solution.

Type Three: Lack-of-resources objections—this objection means that the buyer lacks something: money, time, or authority. The breakdown is in your failure to qualify the buyer fully. Your strategy is to:

- Determine if there is a way to create money. Do you offer financing? Can you accept variable payment schedules? Is there discretionary budget money for you to pursue? Is it a credit problem?
- Is there a way to help your buyer get the time he needs to make the decision? When is the timing better?
- If you're not selling to the real decision maker, can you get to him? Who can say "Yes" to your ideas?

Type Four: Attitude-based objections—attitude-based objections are some of the toughest to deal with. This could be a fear the buyer has for being gouged. It could be that the buyer feels it's risky to pay too much for something. The buyer has some arbitrary upper limit and is committed to not exceeding it. Your strategy is to:

- Demonstrate the greater risk in paying too little for something. Would you price shop when it comes to a child's safety seat or would you want the best?

- The buyer wants to feel good about what he's paying. Reassure him that your prices are in line.
- There are times when a buyer needs permission to indulge himself.

Type Five: Wrong-solution objections—there are times when your solution is too much or too little. Are you selling a sledgehammer to kill a fly? Are you selling a pea shooter to stop a tank? In either case, the buyer feels uncomfortable with your package. You may need to add value or subtract value from your package to suit the buyer's needs.

Type Six: Competition-generated objections—your competition offers the buyer a cheaper price. A reality of price objections is that poor competition exists and they will give away the store. Just because the competition is stupid, you don't want to compound their mistake. Many times when you cut your price you end up cutting your own throat. Your strategy is to:

- Make sure it's an apples-to-apples comparison.
- Is it a bona fide competitive offer?
- Do you want to play the game? Your price may be just fine. Their price is too low. Take Napoleon's advice: Never interrupt an enemy when he's making a mistake.

Discussion Questions

- Why is discounting a costly way to compete?
- What alternatives do you have available to you other than cutting prices?
- Who is the most difficult person for you to negotiate with and why?
- What success have you had in the past by holding the line on prices?
- Name three strategies that will help you deal more effectively with price objections.

TIME MANAGEMENT ATTITUDES

Time is our most precious and fleeting resource. We never have enough yet we have all that there is. This is the time management paradox. Time is something that I feel very passionate about. It's my commodity. I sell it.

Time management is one of these areas where attitude plays a major role in your effectiveness. Attitude drives behavior. We behave as we believe. There are a number of positive time management attitudes that will help you to become more effective.

The Gifts-of-Time Attitude

The gifts-of-time attitude recognizes that every day life hands you moments that collectively turn into hours. Your attitude toward these moments determines your stress level and how you use them. For example, you're in the express line at the grocery store and the person in front of you has two items in his basket that push him over the ten-item limit. How do you handle this? Some people, I call them the shopping line police, feel the need to call attention to the ten-item limit. They say something to the person in front of them. This causes stress and it adds no value to the interaction. Someone with the gifts-of-time attitude will view this unexpected delay as serendipity—a pleasant surprise. This person may use the unexpected gift of time to catch up on reading the point-of-sale magazines. Another person may see this as an opportunity to meet a new friend and strike up a conversation with the person in back of her. And still another person may perceive this as a chance to spend a few minutes with his Creator. These reactions add value to their days.

Your attitude toward time, especially toward these gifts of time, determines the stress level at which you choose to operate. How effectively can you use your time when you feel stress? Do you have the gifts-of-time attitude? Is time your friend or your foe? Does your attitude toward time add value or stress to your day?

Waiting is an attitude. When a customer keeps you waiting for ten or twenty minutes how do you use that time? Some sales-people will sit and stew. Others use that time to prepare and re-view their notes again. It's a gift of time. It's similar to the student who has studied for a test and the teacher announces that there will be a twenty-minute delay before the test begins and that the students may use that time any way they choose. The serious student will spend that last gift of time reviewing what he already knows.

Respect Time

Value added salespeople respect time—their time as well as other people's time. When you respect your time you automati-cally send out signals to others and they too will respect your time. Just because you respect your time doesn't mean that you will disrespect others' time. A healthy respect for your time means that you will make the best use of it. By respecting others' time you acknowledge that you realize their time is as important to them as your time is to you.

Demonstrating a respect for time is especially important in sales. High-level decision makers use time as a weapon. They appreciate the significance of "so many dreams and so little time." For them, time is a precious commodity. You establish credibility with them by mirroring their respect for time.

Be cautious of spending time with customers that seem to have nothing but time. These people ramble and meander incessantly. They are spending your most precious resource. If someone has that much time on his hands aren't you the least bit curious as to why? Maybe he has nothing else going on.

Be Assertive With Your Time

You alone are responsible for how you use your time. No one in this world is more responsible than you for protecting your time. Not your boss. Not your spouse. Not your assistant. You are the most accountable and responsible guardian of your time.

Assertiveness and respect go hand in glove. If you respect your time you will assert yourself when it comes to others misusing your time. If you have difficulty asserting yourself, begin by working on respect for your time. Learn how to say no to people and projects. The world is filled with people that will use your time as a way to get more time for themselves. Some go to great lengths to manipulate others into doing things for them that they should do for themselves.

You cannot please everyone in this world. In fact, there is an emotional disorder reserved for those that try. It's called the please everyone syndrome. If you try to please everyone you generally end up pleasing few—especially yourself. As you attempt to serve others selflessly and tirelessly and work on their priorities versus your priorities you may help them get their work done yet fail to complete your work in the process.

I understand the importance of teamwork and believe in it. I also am leery of people that make it a habit of finding ways to enlist the aid of others to do their work for them. Your ability to sift through different requests and identify legitimate requests to help others will automatically eliminate one of the biggest time wasters all people experience—interruptions.

At this point you are probably thinking, "Boy, this guy Reilly is ruthless when it comes to time." You're right! I am. And I hope to share some of this attitude and respect for time with you. Until you develop a similar "ruthlessness" you will never have enough time to accomplish your goals. Until you develop the habit of prudently saying "No" to others' requests, projects, and priorities you will spend more time working on their objectives than your own. Successful people respect their time and others' time. These people are far more sensitive and accepting to your respectfully declining their requests. At a gut-level they understand the importance of time.

Control Your Time

Do you run your territory or does your territory run you? Do you attack your day or does your day attack you? Are you in control of how you use your time? Most of what happens to you is something over which you have control. Most of what happens is the result of a choice, not chance—the decisions you make and the behaviors in which you engage. Successful time managers control their days as much as possible. They live the philosophy, "If it is to be, it's up to me."

Unsuccessful time managers go through their days by accident. Being in control of your time is starting the day with this question, "What do I want to accomplish today?" Being out of control is beginning your day with the attitude, "Okay phone, ring. Tell me world, what am I supposed to do today?"

There are things in your life that you control and things over which you have little or no control. A simple rule of thumb is to spend time and energy in proportion to the amount of control you have. Those things over which you have maximum control demand more focus and energy on your part. Things over which you have little or no control deserve less focus and energy. Time management is something over which you have significant control. You have a choice as to how to want to invest your time during the day. You can invest it in goal-achieving activities or squander it on non-productive tasks. It is your choice.

Be Proactive With Your Time

Proactive time managers anticipate. They are forward thinkers that take the initiative and act. Reactive time managers have a wait-and-see attitude. They live life a day at a time. They are more focused on responding than initiating. A proactive approach to time management is goal achieving. A reactive approach is more crises relieving. Proactive time managers control their days. Reactive time managers relinquish some control to their days. Proactive time managers prevent fires. Reactive time managers fight fires.

There is a fundamental question that you can ask yourself daily to adopt a more proactive attitude toward time management, "What can I do today to stay ahead of the game?" This shifts your focus to the future. It encourages you to plan and take the initiative. By being proactive you ensure that you are working on your priorities versus someone else's priorities. You are staging activities that keep you on the path of goal achievement. You are running your day versus your day running you.

Good time management is good self-management. You manage your behavior within the constraints of time. Everyone has time management habits—effective or not. To become a more effective self and time manager, focus on priorities that add value to your day. Remember, time is your most precious resource. Invest it in ways that will help you to create the life you want to live.

Value Added Time Management

Good time management is good self-management. You manage your behavior within the constraints of time. Everyone has time management habits—effective or not. To become a more effective self and time manager, focus on priorities that add value to your day. Remember, time is your most precious resource. Invest it in ways that will help you to create the life you want to live. Do more of that which adds value to your life and less of that which adds little or no value to your life.

Discussion Questions

- How do you currently set priorities?
- What are your biggest time wasters?
- Are you as effective? Why or why not?
- Describe your weekly planning process.
- What three things can you do to manage your time?

Speaker. Author. Business owner. Salesman. Tom Reilly is the guy who literally wrote the book on *Value-Added Selling*. Tom's sales career began with a Fortune 500 chemical company where, in his first full year in sales, Tom earned his company's award as *Salesman-of-the-year*.

Tom eventually left this company to start his own chemical company in Houston, Texas. In 1981, Tom sold his company to begin a career as a full-time professional speaker. In 1985, wrote his first book on *Value-Added Selling*. Since then, Tom has written a total of ten business books and is one of the most sought-after speakers globally on selling value.

Tom's motto is: "Add value, not cost; sell value, not price!" Tom has shared his content-rich message of hope with more than 100,000 salespeople, sales managers and customer service representatives in every industry. Tom has a Bachelor's and Master's Degree in psychology with a special emphasis in motivation theory. He addresses corporate and association audiences in addition to conducting public seminars at his training center in Chesterfield, Missouri.

You can visit Tom's website to learn more about his other books and seminars: www.TomReillyTraining.com

Tom Reilly's Books and Tapes

Value-Added Selling (also available on four-CD set)

Crush Price Objections (also available on cassette tape)

**Customer Service Is More Than a Department:
It's an Attitude**

**Coaching for Sales Success:
How to Create the Value Added Sales Culture**

Get Out of the Wagon and Help Me Pull This Thing
(a leadership parable)

Value Added Sales Management

Selling Smart!

Simple Psychology: Simple Living in a Complex World

Value Added Time Management (CD)

The Value Added Organization (Book and video series)

For more information: www.TomReillyTraining.com